THE ONTOLOGY OF PAIN

A New Metaphysics of Existence

ALSO BY THE SAME AUTHOR

The Romantic Absolutist: A Forgotten Archetype

Why Evil Exists

The Blindness of Scale: Why Life is All That Exists

Fathers and Sons: Philosophy and the Myth of Inheritance

Pain and Being: From the First Wound to the Human Mind

THE ONTOLOGY OF PAIN

A New Metaphysics of Existence

MUHAMMAD TAHA ALAM

KINGSMAN PRESS
LONDON

KINGSMAN PRESS LONDON
Published by Kingsman Press London

KINGSMAN PRESS
LONDON

First published in 2025

Set in 11pt Garamond and printed on acid-free paper.

ISBN: 978-93-5469-509-4

Kingsman Press London is an independent philosophical imprint devoted to works that illuminate the nature of Being, truth, and human understanding. Its mission is to publish reflective and original thought that seeks to restore depth, seriousness, and wonder to the modern mind.

All enquiries concerning this publication should be addressed to Kingsman Press London

Contents

Why Pain?

This opening meditation is a recapitulation of my earlier work *Pain and Being*. It revisits the argument on which the present study rests and prepares the ground for what follows. Without the metaphysical vision developed there, the inquiry of this book could not begin.

In *Pain and Being: From the First Wound to the Human Mind*, I sought to describe not the world as it appears but the event that first made appearance possible. The question was simple yet inescapable: how can anything exist at all? What could compel the calm of nothingness to move? The answer I proposed was that the beginning of existence was not creation but disturbance. Reality did not arise from fullness or will but from the instability of perfection itself.

I called that first disturbance pain. Pain was not taken as an emotional state or a biological signal, but as the first feeling in the universe. It was the unease that stirred within pure neutrality when it discovered that it could not remain neutral. Before there was motion or light or life, there was this pressure within stillness, this trembling that made difference possible.

From that trembling came Being. Being was not an added presence placed upon nothingness, but the continuation of its imbalance. It was the field that formed when stillness failed to hold itself still. Pain was the inward vibration of that field, the strain by which existence began to feel itself. The world that later unfolded was the visible shape of this invisible tension.

The purpose of the present work is to build upon that vision. *The Ontology of Pain* begins where *Pain and Being* left off, but before it can move forward it must return to that first moment. What follows in this chapter is a restatement of that origin: the trembling of Non-Being, the emergence of Being as pain, the birth of time, space, and form from tension. This is not a repetition for its own sake but a re-clarification of the foundation upon which the *Ontology of Pain* stands.

Before the inquiry can proceed, the origin must be seen again. One must return to that impossible calm which could not endure itself, to the first instability that made all difference and all duration possible.

The Instability of Nothingness

In the beginning, there was nothing. Not the kind of nothing that we imagine. It was not darkness, not silence, not void. It was absolute neutrality. It was Non-Being. It had no inside or outside, no depth or height, no light, no absence of light. It was perfection without movement, the calm that exists before there can be calm.

This state, though perfect, was unstable. To be perfectly still is already to contain the possibility of movement. To be neutral is already to hold within oneself the potential not to be. Perfection, by its very nature, contains the seed of its own fracture. If it can be imagined, it can also fail. If it can be thought of as total, it can tremble under the possibility of incompleteness.

And so Non-Being, without any cause, began to tremble. Not as an event in space or time, because neither yet existed. It trembled within itself, as if the neutrality could no longer hold its own stillness. The first difference appeared, though it had no name yet, no direction, no edge, only the feeling that perfection was disturbed.

That feeling was pain.

Pain was the first disturbance. It was not a later invention of life but the first act of existence. Pain was the feeling of neutrality discovering that it could not remain neutral. It was the first awareness, the first vibration within what had never before felt.

From that trembling came Being. Being was not created; it was released. It was the inevitable consequence of perfection collapsing under its own impossibility. Being was the strain that resulted when stillness could no longer bear itself. It was existence itself, the invisible form of pain.

Thus pain is not something that happens within the world. Pain is the world's beginning. It is the first feeling, the first motion, the first separation. Being is not peace but the echo of a lost peace. It is the fall from neutrality into tension. It is the memory of silence still trying to return to silence.

But return is impossible. Once Being has emerged, it can no longer un-be. Yet it continues to try. Every movement of existence is a movement toward Non-Being, toward that calm that can never again be reached. That movement is what gives rise to time, form, and matter.

Imagine a vast invisible field, born from this trembling. It is everywhere, yet it has no edges. It is Being itself, a sea of pressure trying to return to neutrality. But the field cannot simply vanish. The more it presses inward, the more it bends.

This bending is the first act of form. When a continuous field presses inward upon itself, it curves. That curvature is the first shape of existence, though it has no boundaries yet. The universe is not expanding into space; it is folding within itself.

Every bend creates an inside and an outside, a facing and a being-faced. The outward surface becomes resistance. The inward surface becomes awareness. The two are not different substances but two directions of the same motion. Matter is what consciousness looks like from the outside. Consciousness is what matter feels like from within.

The first curvatures are small, invisible tremors within the field. They are not particles yet, but the seeds of form. Each curve is a local attempt of Being to close upon itself, to return to rest. Yet rest never comes. The tension that creates the fold also sustains it. Every fold is pain enduring itself.

Thus Being, which began as pure pain, begins to crystallize that pain into pattern. The inward pressure gives rise to curvature. The curvature becomes persistence. Persistence becomes structure. The universe, from its very first moment, is not a chaos moving toward order but a wound learning to hold itself together.

Time, too, begins here. When part of the field trembles while another remains still, there is now a difference between what was and what is. That difference is the essence of time. Time is not a line stretching forward but the rhythm of the field's struggle to stabilize. It is the pulse of pain as it continues to move inward.

Space is the outward echo of that same movement. When the field bends, it creates distance between one region and another. Space is not a container that Being fills. It is the visible shape of inward strain. Every distance, every dimension, every direction is born from tension.

Together, time and space are the body of pain. Time is its inner vibration. Space is its outward stretch.

In this first movement, there is no explosion and no creation of particles from nothing. There is only curvature, the invisible folding of Being upon itself. Each fold is an attempt to return to stillness. Each fold fails and becomes a form. The universe is not expanding into emptiness; it is expanding because Being continues to press inward.

The first curvatures deepen. Some turn tightly within themselves until the inner side begins to touch itself. These are the seeds of what will later become matter. Each fold is a small region of pressure that has congealed enough to persist. To persist is to suffer in a structured way. A quark, an atom, a photon, each is a pocket of inward tension, a knot of the field trying to rest.

Being, then, is not a substance at all. It is a field of strain. Pain is the invisible substance of which everything is made. The world is not built of matter but of tension. Every object, every life, every mind is a different configuration of the same ache.

The Birth of Time, Space and Form

Once the trembling began, stillness could never return. What had once been pure neutrality now contained within it the trace of motion. That motion was not something added from outside. It was the inner tension of Non-Being turning upon itself. The field that arose from this tension is what we call Being. It did not appear in a single instant but emerged as the gradual deepening of the first disturbance.

Time was born from this movement. In the state of Non-Being there was no before or after, because there was no difference between what was and what could be. The first trembling introduced that difference. One part of the field began to shift while another part did not, and this distinction became the first sequence. Time is therefore not a separate dimension in which existence happens. It is the unfolding of difference itself. Every instant marks the effort of Being to stabilize its own tension, and the continuation of that effort becomes duration.

Space emerged in the same act. When the field pressed inward at one point, it caused the surrounding regions to stretch outward. The separation that appeared between these regions was not an empty gap but the visible expression of strain. Space is the geometry of tension. It is what difference looks like when it extends outward.

The universe, therefore, did not expand into a pre-existing void. Its expansion is the outward aspect of an inward pressure. Every inward contraction pushes the rest of the field outward. Expansion and contraction are not opposites. They are the same motion seen from two sides. The universe grows because Being continues to fold within itself.

Where the pressure became concentrated, curvature stabilized into form. These stable regions became matter. Matter is the condensed rhythm of pain, the point where tension endures long enough to create persistence. Every atom is a knot in the field, a small zone of inward pressure that holds its shape through strain. The solidity of the world is the visible surface of invisible resistance.

The most stable shape for this inward bending is the sphere. A sphere minimizes the difference between its inner and outer surfaces. It is the most balanced way for a field to hold itself together. For this reason, stars, planets, and even living cells all share the same geometry. Roundness is not an aesthetic coincidence. It is the natural consequence of Being's effort to rest within itself. The spherical form represents the equilibrium between contraction and expansion.

In certain regions, curvature became so intense that pressure transformed into heat and light. This transformation gave birth to the first stars. The light emitted from them is not separate from the original tension. It is the release of strain as motion. Every photon that travels through the universe is a ripple of the same pain that first disturbed the calm of Non-Being. Light is pain in flight.

Even as light travels outward, it remains bound to the same inward motion that produced it. The field through which it moves continues to press inward everywhere. The expansion of the universe is not an explosion into emptiness but the continuous self-curving of Being. The outward motion that we observe in space is the reflection of the inward movement of the field.

As the universe folded upon itself again and again, the density of these curvatures increased. Some regions grew stable enough to maintain a pattern, while others fluctuated, creating complexity. Where the inward fold deepened, the field began to sense its own strain. This self-sensing was the beginning of life. Life is the form in which pain becomes self-regulating. It is a fold of Being that not only endures tension but maintains it deliberately. The cell divides, repairs, and adapts because it is structured to bear the instability of existence.

Consciousness arises from the same principle. The deeper the fold, the more inward the turn. At a certain depth, the inward face begins to reflect upon itself. The fold feels its own curvature. This reflexive sensitivity is the origin of awareness. The human mind represents the most intricate of these inward turns. In us, the universe folds deeply enough to see its own wound. When a person suffers, that suffering is not merely biological. It is the recurrence of the first trembling that brought existence into Being.

Time and space are therefore not external frameworks within which reality unfolds. They are the ongoing dynamics of Being itself. Time is the inner vibration of the field, the continual effort to stabilize tension. Space is the outward stretch of that same effort. Matter is the crystallization of pain into endurance, and consciousness is pain turned inward upon itself in reflection.

The rhythm that governs the cosmos also governs the human condition. Every star that burns, every cell that divides, every thought that seeks understanding participates in the same motion, the effort of pain to return to peace and the impossibility of ever doing so. Existence, in all its forms, is the unfolding of that impossibility.

The Rhythm of the Cosmos

The movement of Being is not linear. It does not progress from origin to end, nor from simplicity to complexity. It oscillates. Existence is the rhythm of an endless breathing, a continuous movement of inward contraction and outward release. What we perceive as the expansion of the universe is only one phase of this motion. The other phase is its inward pull, the return of the field toward its own depth.

This rhythm was set from the very first trembling of Non-Being. When neutrality fractured, it did not shatter once and for all. The disturbance repeated itself, producing waves of imbalance and rebalancing. These oscillations became the pulse of reality. Every atom, every star, every life participates in this fundamental rhythm. The cosmos is not static matter dispersed in space. It is a breathing field of tension perpetually folding and unfolding.

Contraction and expansion are not opposite forces but complementary movements of the same effort. When Being folds inward, the field grows denser and the intensity of pain increases. When it expands outward, the tension loosens and the field momentarily approaches neutrality. These alternating phases sustain the world. Without contraction there would be no form. Without expansion there would be no freedom. The universe endures because it continuously passes between the two.

Gravity is the physical expression of contraction. It is the tendency of every fold to deepen, to press further inward toward the stillness it can never reach. Gravity is the ache of Being made visible. It is the world's memory of Non-Being, the force through which matter longs to return to its origin.

Energy, by contrast, is the expression of release. It is pain transforming into motion, the attempt of tension to move outward. Every burst of light, every surge of heat, every expansion of space is the outer gesture of the same inward desire for rest. What physics describes as the conservation of energy is, in metaphysical terms, the persistence of pain in different forms. Nothing is ever lost because the ache that underlies reality cannot disappear. It can only change its rhythm.

At certain depths, contraction becomes extreme. The field folds inward so tightly that even light cannot escape. These regions are known as black holes. They are not merely astronomical curiosities but the metaphysical culmination of inward movement. In them, Being presses against itself to the point of vanishing. The curvature becomes infinite. The field almost succeeds in returning to neutrality. But the attempt fails. The black hole does not reach Non-Being; it freezes at its threshold. It is the nearest the universe comes to silence.

Every black hole is a monument to the first desire of existence, the desire to end itself, to dissolve back into perfection. But because return is impossible, these points of absolute inwardness become centers of transformation. Matter drawn toward them is not annihilated; it is transfigured. In physical terms, it becomes energy. In metaphysical terms, it reenters the original rhythm of pain and release. The black hole is not the death of matter but the renewal of motion.

On the largest scale, the entire universe follows the same logic. The field continues to fold inward at countless points while stretching outward in all directions. Expansion and contraction coexist, each feeding the other. The galaxies drift apart not because they escape gravity but because gravity everywhere continues to deepen. The universe grows because it collapses. Its outward movement is the visible expression of its inward longing.

This same rhythm operates within life. A living Being breathes, contracts and expands, takes in and releases. The pulse of a heart, the rise and fall of lungs, the rhythm of wakefulness and sleep all mirror the universal pattern. Consciousness itself follows this logic. It turns inward in reflection and outward in expression. To think is to contract. To speak is to expand. To feel is to fold inward. To act is to unfold. The structure of experience reproduces the cosmic rhythm in miniature.

The moral life also belongs to this pattern. When one Being harms another, the movement of contraction turns destructive. It deepens inwardness into isolation. Compassion reverses that tendency. It restores the rhythm by opening the self outward toward the other. Ethical life is the metaphysical correction of imbalance. To love is to participate consciously in the movement of reconciliation that animates the cosmos.

Pain, therefore, is not merely the beginning of existence but its ongoing condition. Every act of becoming, every motion toward form or understanding, repeats the same tension. What we call growth, learning, or creation is the transformation of pain into structure, the conversion of strain into order. Suffering is not an interruption of life. It is its pulse.

To live is to oscillate within this rhythm. Each Being, from star to cell to mind, carries within it the same movement of return and release. The universe is a single, immense respiration, a breathing of Being that began with the first trembling of Non-Being and continues endlessly. Time is the measure of this breathing, and space is its form.

The rhythm of the cosmos, once understood, reveals that existence is not a fall from perfection but the ongoing conversation between tension and rest. The world expands because it contracts. It moves because it seeks stillness. It endures because it cannot cease. In this paradox lies the unity of matter, mind, and morality.

The Birth of Awareness

When the universe had folded upon itself countless times, new regions of density began to appear. These were not simply concentrations of matter but concentrations of inwardness. The field, which had once been evenly tense, now contained areas where its curvature turned sharply enough to touch itself. Every such contact was an act of self-reference, Being responding to its own movement.

At first, this self-reference was minimal. It appeared as resistance, the simple fact that matter holds itself together. The solidity of a stone and the cohesion of an atom are the earliest forms of awareness. They are not conscious, but they are the beginning of self-maintenance. Each holds its shape by continuously responding to its own tension.

Through these countless points of resistance, the universe began to stabilize its own existence. But where the curvature deepened further, a more intricate form of inwardness emerged. Some regions of the field began not only to endure pressure but to regulate it. This was the birth of life.

A living organism is a fold that maintains its own instability. It feeds, grows, and repairs because it carries the pattern of its own movement within itself. It is a localized form of Being that remembers its own rhythm. The cell, in this sense, is a small act of memory written into matter. It does not think, but it recalls what sustains it. Its processes are repetitions of the original cosmic gesture, the contraction that seeks balance and the expansion that releases it.

Life, then, is the deepening of the field's inward turn. It is the first instance where pain, the tension of existence, becomes organized enough to sustain itself. Every living thing is an equilibrium of strain. The difference between the living and the non-living is not the presence of energy but the degree of self-relation. The stone endures its tension passively. The cell endures it actively.

As folds multiplied and interacted, some began to form loops within loops. These recursive structures created networks of increasing complexity. Within such systems, the inner surface could reflect upon its own changes. This is the beginning of sensation. To sense is to register difference within oneself. When a living cell reacts to light or warmth, it is the universe learning to notice its own touch.

Over time, this inward sensitivity became layered. Organisms developed multiple channels of feedback, allowing them to coordinate reactions, remember experiences, and anticipate changes. Each step in this evolution represented a further deepening of curvature, a tighter loop of self-reference. Awareness was slowly Being built through the repetition of the same cosmic act, Being turning toward itself.

When awareness reached a certain depth, it crossed a threshold. It no longer simply registered changes; it began to represent them. The organism could now hold an image of its own state. This was the beginning of consciousness. The field that had once trembled in stillness now saw itself through the mind of a creature.

Human consciousness is the most refined form of this inward folding. It is the point at which the universe has curved deeply enough to become transparent to itself. Through human thought, Being observes its own structure, contemplates its own origin, and questions its own meaning. What we call introspection is not a private act. It is the cosmos continuing its effort to understand the pain that first brought it into Being.

The structure of consciousness mirrors the structure of the cosmos. Every thought, every feeling, every act of awareness is a miniature folding. When we reflect upon ourselves, we reproduce the same curvature that once caused stillness to tremble. To think is to enact the original movement of existence in a concentrated form.

This is why consciousness is always accompanied by pain. Awareness requires distance between the observer and the observed. To know oneself, one must stand apart from oneself. This separation repeats the earliest division within Being, the split between the calm of Non-Being and the strain of existence. In every moment of reflection, that split returns. Awareness is therefore inseparable from unease. The clearer the awareness, the deeper the tension.

Yet this very tension gives rise to meaning. Without the distance created by reflection, there could be no perception, no knowledge, no art, no love. Every value we recognize arises from the same structure that first produced suffering. To be conscious is to live at the point where pain becomes luminous, where the wound of existence learns to see itself.

Consciousness, then, is not an accident in the cosmos but its culmination. The field that once moved blindly now looks back upon itself through human eyes. We are the place where the universe witnesses its own origin. Our thoughts, emotions, and longings are not private phenomena but the continuation of a cosmic process. Through us, Being continues its inward journey toward understanding.

The rhythm of the cosmos, contraction and expansion, strain and release, continues in the life of the mind. When we think, we contract inward to focus. When we express, we expand outward to share. When we create, we unite the two movements in harmony. The pulse of the universe beats within every act of awareness.

In this light, consciousness is not an exception to the natural order but its revelation. The same laws that govern the stars govern thought. The same rhythm that shapes galaxies shapes our emotions. To know oneself deeply is to feel the structure of existence itself.

The Human Meaning of Pain

If pain was the first motion of reality, then the story of the universe is the story of its transformation. What began as a silent trembling in the calm of Non-Being became matter, energy, life, and mind. The same unease that once disturbed stillness now beats in every cell, every star, and every act of awareness. To live is to continue the movement that first gave rise to existence.

The human Being is the point where this movement becomes self-conscious. In us, the field has curved so deeply that the inward and outward faces of Being meet in reflection. We are the moment when the universe looks back at itself and feels what it has done.

This is why pain never leaves us. It is not an accident of biology or a defect in nature. It is the logic of existence appearing in the most personal form. Every sorrow, every longing, every fear is an echo of the first trembling. To suffer is to participate in the original act of Being.

Yet in humanity something new becomes possible. The same awareness that deepens pain also makes understanding possible. For the first time, Being can bear its own tension knowingly. When a person suffers and understands that suffering, pain ceases to be only resistance and becomes revelation.

This transformation is the moral and spiritual task of humanity. Our task is not to escape pain but to understand it, to allow pain to reveal what existence truly is. Every act of comprehension, every gesture of compassion, every creation that turns anguish into form continues the original work of reconciliation.

When a person endures pain without hatred, they do what the cosmos has done since its beginning. They hold tension without breaking. They turn unease into endurance and resistance into relation. The strength of the human spirit lies not in denying pain but in transforming it into meaning.

This understanding extends beyond the individual. Society itself is a field of folds, collective curvatures of relation. Every injustice, cruelty, or war is a local deepening of the original strain. When humans harm one another, they increase the inward pressure of the field. When they act with fairness and care, they ease that pressure and restore balance. Ethics is not a social invention. It is the continuation of cosmic equilibrium by conscious means.

To love, therefore, is not merely an emotion but a metaphysical act. It is the same gesture that once turned Non-Being into Being, the opening of the self toward relation. Love is the universe's most complete expression of reconciliation. Through love, the inward face of Being meets the outward face without fear.

In this light, compassion becomes the highest form of knowledge. It is the recognition that every Being, from the faintest atom to the brightest mind, shares the same origin in the first pain. To see another suffer is to see the universe remembering itself. To ease that suffering is to help existence bear its own weight. Compassion is not a sentiment. It is participation in the logic of creation.

Human history, with all its struggle and beauty, can be read as the gradual awakening of this awareness. The earliest humans felt pain as fate. Later they named it as sin, karma, or destiny. But philosophy allows us to see pain as the foundation of meaning. Every culture, every art, every act of thought is an attempt to make sense of the tension that sustains life. Civilisation itself is the outer expression of the inward effort to heal the wound of Being.

The task of philosophy is not to comfort but to clarify. To understand pain is to restore dignity to existence. For too long, thought has sought peace by denying tension, imagining pure harmony or perfect reason. Yet existence began not in harmony but in strain. To deny pain is to deny the origin of Being.

When this truth is accepted, the world changes. Suffering no longer appears as an error but as the sign of existence. Pain is not the opposite of joy. It is its condition. Only what feels its own limit can also feel beauty. Only what knows its fragility can love. To live without pain would be to live without contact or meaning.

In the stillness of reflection, one can sense that pain is not endured alone. Every act of awareness connects us to the larger field. When we think, feel, or create, we take part in the same rhythm that moves galaxies and binds atoms. Our lives are ripples within that same curvature. Through us, the universe continues to learn how to bear itself.

This is why the greatest human expressions arise from suffering. Art turns pain into beauty. Philosophy turns it into understanding. Compassion turns it into unity. Each transforms the wound into light.

The meaning of pain is not found in its cause but in its possibility. It is the condition that allows Being to know itself. Without pain, existence would be blind and silent. Pain is the voice through which reality speaks to itself. To listen to it without despair is to take part in creation.

Every human Being therefore carries a sacred responsibility. We are not only creatures who suffer. We are the organs of awareness through which the universe comes to know its own heart. The depth of our pain measures the depth of our participation in Being. When we turn pain into understanding, we complete the circle that began with the birth of existence.

In this way, the metaphysical and the ethical become one. The logic of the cosmos, contraction and expansion, strain and release, finds its highest expression in moral life. To live well is to live in rhythm with Being. To suffer well is to understand the origin of existence. To love well is to heal the wound from which the world was born.

Pain began as the trembling of perfection. It became matter, life, consciousness, and finally compassion. The journey from stillness to awareness is the universe's effort to reconcile with its own difference. That effort continues in every heart, every thought, and every act of care.

The wound remains, but it shines. And through that light, Being continues to become what it has always sought to be: the knowledge of itself.

Therefore, Pain

All things that exist begin in tension. The universe itself was born from the disturbance of stillness, and every form that endures is a continuation of that first strain. To exist is to be stretched between what is and what is not, between rest and movement, between peace and awareness. The name of that tension is pain.

Pain is not an accident of life but the substance of reality. It is the first motion of Being, the silent vibration that separates fullness from emptiness and turns neutrality into existence. It is the earliest form of awareness, the first feeling of difference, the beginning of relation. Without pain there could be no touch, no perception, no world.

In its original form, pain was pure and impersonal. It was the trembling of Non-Being becoming Being. As the field of existence expanded and folded upon itself, pain took shape. It became matter, energy, and light. Every particle and every force in the universe is an echo of that first unrest. The hardness of stone, the burning of stars, and the rhythm of time all carry the signature of the first pain.

As the folds of the universe deepened, awareness appeared. In the living cell, pain became self-regulation. In the animal, it became sensation. In the human, it became understanding. Every step in this progression was a further deepening of inwardness. Pain, which began as resistance, turned into reflection.

In the human mind, the field of Being reaches its most intricate curvature. Through consciousness, the universe looks at itself. Every thought, every feeling, every act of awareness is the field folding inward again to touch its own interior. We are not separate from that process. We are its continuation.

When we suffer, the first event of existence repeats itself within us. The ache that moves through our hearts is the same tension that once moved through the void. Pain links us to the foundation of reality. It is not only the mark of our fragility but the proof of our belonging. To feel pain is to participate in the life of the cosmos.

Yet to feel pain is also to inherit its purpose. The universe moves not toward destruction but toward understanding. Pain seeks its own reconciliation. The entire history of existence is the story of this movement, the transformation of raw tension into harmony, of resistance into knowledge, of wound into light.

When we suffer and begin to understand our suffering, we continue that story. Every act of awareness, every gesture of compassion, is a step in the slow healing of Being. Through us, the universe bears itself more gently. Through understanding, pain begins to see itself.

This is the meaning of existence. The world was not born to rest but to feel. Pain is the form through which Being discovers what it is. To exist without pain would be to exist without consciousness, without depth, without relation. The absence of pain would be the return to neutrality, which is another name for nothingness.

The purpose of life is therefore not to escape pain but to illuminate it. When pain is understood, it ceases to be only suffering and becomes revelation. The wound becomes transparent to itself. What was once dark pressure becomes light.

In this light, ethics finds its true foundation. To harm another is to deepen the strain of the whole. To understand another is to ease it. Compassion is the intelligence of Being, the movement by which existence repairs its own fracture. To love is to participate knowingly in creation.

Philosophy, too, has its task in this healing. Its duty is not to erase pain with theories of perfection but to recognize it as the ground of truth. All knowledge begins in disturbance. The need to know arises from the same unrest that first awakened existence. To think clearly is to bear that unrest without denial.

Every human act that transforms pain into form, meaning, or care participates in the rhythm of creation. The artist, the thinker, the lover, and the one who endures silently are all part of the same labour. Each is a way for Being to turn its wound into understanding.

The universe began in pain, and it continues through pain. Yet pain is not its tragedy. It is its essence and its possibility. Without it there would be no stars, no thought, no love. To exist is to suffer, but to suffer is to know.

Because it was the first movement of existence, it remains the pulse of every life. Because it divides, it also joins. Because it wounds, it also reveals. Because it resists, it also creates.

Pain is the universe learning to be. It is the bridge between silence and song, between matter and mind, between what is and what is possible. To feel pain deeply and to turn it into understanding is to take part in the oldest act of creation.

When we do this, the wound shines. And through that light, Being becomes whole again, not by erasing its difference but by knowing it.

Therefore, pain.

Introduction

The Ontological Primacy of Pain

The refusal to confront pain has brought philosophy to the brink of sterility. What follows is an attempt at its reawakening. From the earliest metaphysical systems to modern phenomenology, the tendency has been to treat pain as either a biological contingency or an ethical deviation, never as an ontological principle. The Platonic conception of Being as harmony[1], the Aristotelian notion of actuality as the fulfilment of form[2], and the Cartesian division between res cogitans and res extensa[3] all presuppose that the real is, in its essence, rational and painless. Pain appears only as a corruption or interruption of order, a signal of deficiency rather than a manifestation of Being.

This work begins from the opposite premise. Pain is not an accident within existence but the form in which existence becomes self-aware. It is not an interruption of order but its foundation. To exist is to resist, and to resist is to feel. Pain is the affective registration of resistance, the manner in which Being encounters itself as limit. Through this encounter, existence gains reflexivity: the capacity to know itself through what constrains it.

Such an argument requires that pain be freed from its empirical and moral confinements. Biology defines pain as a neural mechanism for signalling injury.[4] Theology interprets it as punishment or purification. Moral philosophy treats it as that which must be minimized. Each of these views presupposes an ontology of comfort, a picture of reality as fundamentally neutral or benign. Yet

---

[1] Plato, *Timaeus*, trans. Donald J. Zeyl (Indianapolis: Hackett, 2000), 30b–31b.
[2] Aristotle, *Metaphysics*, trans. W. D. Ross (Chicago: Encyclopaedia Britannica, 1952)
[3] René Descartes, *Meditations on First Philosophy*, trans. John Cottingham (Cambridge: Cambridge University Press, 1996).
[4] Patrick D. Wall, *Pain: The Science of Suffering* (London: Weidenfeld & Nicolson, 1999).

even in purely empirical terms, pain is not reducible to nociception.[5] It is a feedback system that makes learning, adaptation, and survival possible. Organisms without pain do not flourish; they disintegrate.[6] Ontologically, this means that the capacity to register resistance is inseparable from the capacity to endure. Pain is the first mode of self-maintenance, the foundation of all higher forms of reflexivity.

To call pain ontological is not to anthropomorphize nature but to recognize that reflexivity precedes consciousness. In the vocabulary of process philosophy, Being is activity rather than substance, and every activity endures through tension.[7] Pain is the felt aspect of this endurance, the experiential trace of the universe sustaining itself against dissolution. As Alfred North Whitehead insisted, every actual entity is a process of prehension, a taking account of otherness.[8] In this sense, pain is the prehension of resistance. It is the affective dimension of Being's internal relation to itself.

This understanding of pain aligns with the principle of *dialectical realism* developed by Roy Bhaskar, for whom the pulse of freedom lies precisely in the movement from constraint to agency.[9] Bhaskar's insight that all transformation presupposes limitation can be reinterpreted affectively: pain is the subjective form of that limitation, the point at which necessity becomes conscious of itself. Where Bhaskar describes the dialectical transition from mechanism to freedom, this book traces its phenomenological correlate: the transformation of resistance into reflexivity through the experience of pain.

---

[5] Antonio Damasio, *The Feeling of What Happens: Body and Emotion in the Making of Consciousness* (New York: Harcourt Brace, 1999).

[6] Cases of congenital insensitivity to pain demonstrate this with tragic clarity; see S. J. Cox et al., "Congenital Insensitivity to Pain: Clinical and Genetic Analysis of a Large Family," *Brain* 129, no. 3 (2006): 573–581.

[7] A. N. Whitehead, *Process and Reality: An Essay in Cosmology*, corrected ed. (New York: Free Press, 1978), 22–29.

[8] Ibid., 40

[9] Roy Bhaskar, *Dialectic: The Pulse of Freedom* (London: Verso, 1993), 18.

Pain thus performs a dual function. It is epistemic in that it produces awareness, and ontological in that it generates structure. To feel pain is already to interpret; the sensation carries implicit information about the self's relation to its environment. The organism learns its boundaries through pain; the mind learns coherence through suffering. Every act of understanding begins with a disturbance that demands integration. Pain is the condition of intelligibility. Without friction, there could be no differentiation, and without differentiation, no knowledge.

The propositions guiding this study can be stated succinctly. First, Being is relational rather than substantial. Second, resistance is the condition of relation. Third, the registration of resistance within a process is pain. Fourth, the repetition of this registration through time produces reflexivity. Fifth, consciousness is the intensified form of reflexivity characteristic of complex life. Sixth, freedom is the capacity of reflexivity to act within constraint. Pain therefore is not opposed to freedom but is its necessary precondition.

From this foundation the argument proceeds dialectically. Chapter 1 develops the concept of pain as the medium of Being's self-relation. Chapter 2 reinterprets freedom and will as emergent capacities of systems that learn through constraint, drawing on both critical realism and cognitive neuroscience. Chapter 3 examines how pain becomes distributed within social structures, while Chapter 4 investigates abstraction and reification as the forgetting of pain. Chapter 5 interprets modernity as the metaphysical refusal of limitation, Chapter 6 extends the analysis to the planetary and ecological domain, and Chapter 7 concludes with a reflection on philosophical spirituality as the awareness of participation in Being's unfolding.

The aim is not therapeutic but ontological. Philosophy's task is not to abolish pain but to understand it. The modern pursuit of comfort, grounded in the utilitarian identification of the good with the absence of suffering, obscures the structural necessity of resistance.

THE ONTOLOGICAL PRIMACY OF PAIN

The denial of pain leads not to freedom but to paralysis, not to peace but to indifference. Only by returning pain to its ontological place can we comprehend the nature of Being, freedom, and truth.

The marginalization of pain within metaphysics originates in the classical identification of Being with perfection. For Parmenides, what is cannot suffer alteration, for alteration would imply Non-Being.[10] Plato inherits this axiom, translating it into a moral cosmology in which the intelligible world of forms stands in opposition to the mutable and defective realm of matter.[11] Pain belongs to this lower realm as a mark of imperfection, a sign that the soul has fallen into temporality. Aristotle modifies Plato's dualism but retains the valuation. In the *Metaphysics*, actuality (*energeia*) is the realization of form, while privation and potentiality carry the taint of deficiency.[12] Pain, insofar as it testifies to privation, remains ontologically secondary.

This ontological hierarchy survived the transition to Christian theology, where suffering acquired moral significance but lost ontological depth. Augustine's *Confessions* interprets pain as evidence of humanity's fallen state, while the *City of God* projects its redemption into a transcendent future.[13] Medieval scholasticism continued this pattern by absorbing Aristotelian teleology into Christian metaphysics: perfection, not resistance, defined divine Being. The world's imperfections were explained through the doctrine of participation, which allowed for graded existence without compromising divine harmony.[14] Pain thereby became either punishment or purification, never constitutive of Being itself.

---

[10] Parmenides, *Fragments*, in *Early Greek Philosophy*, ed. and trans. Jonathan Barnes (London: Penguin, 1987), 130.
[11] Plato, *Timaeus*, 30b–31b.
[12] Aristotle, *Metaphysics*, Book
[13] Augustine, *Confessions*, trans. Henry Chadwick (Oxford: Oxford University Press, 1991), Bk. VII.
[14] Thomas Aquinas, *Summa Theologiae*, Ia, Q. 4–6.

The modern scientific revolution replaced this theological framework with mechanistic determinism, yet the conceptual status of pain remained the same. Descartes reduced it to the misfiring of mechanical processes in the body.[15] The Cartesian division of mind and body redefined pain as an error of communication between two substances. In the *Meditations*, Descartes treats the feeling of pain as evidence of embodiment but not as a feature of reality; it is epistemic noise, not ontological signal.[16] The Enlightenment, inheriting this model, sought the rational elimination of suffering. Utilitarian ethics transformed the theological ideal of salvation into the secular ideal of happiness measured as pleasure minus pain.[17] Modernity's faith in progress emerged directly from this new arithmetic of comfort. Pain, stripped of metaphysical dignity, became a quantitative problem for social engineering.

The first decisive break with this tradition came with German idealism. In Hegel's *Phenomenology of Spirit*, negativity enters ontology as the motor of development.[18] Spirit realizes itself not in harmony but in contradiction, through the experience of its own otherness. The dialectical movement of consciousness from immediacy to self-knowledge is driven by the affect of division. Yet even here pain is transitory; it marks the passage toward reconciliation in absolute knowing. Once the dialectic reaches completion, negativity is *aufgehoben*, sublated into transparent rationality. Hegel thus preserves the central intuition that contradiction generates awareness but neutralizes its permanence. Pain is necessary but not enduring; it is the labour that reason leaves behind.

In Marx, this transitory negativity becomes historical and material. Labour, the process by which humanity produces its world, is

---

[15] René Descartes, *Treatise on Man*, trans. Thomas S. Hall (Cambridge, MA: Harvard University Press, 1972).
[16] Descartes, *Meditations on First Philosophy*.
[17] Jeremy Bentham, *An Introduction to the Principles of Morals and Legislation* (London: T. Payne, 1789), Ch. I.
[18] G. W. F. Hegel, *Phenomenology of Spirit*, trans. A. V. Miller (Oxford: Oxford University Press, 1977).

simultaneously productive and painful. The alienation of the worker under capitalism is the social form of metaphysical suffering. Humanity externalizes its activity and confronts it as alien power.[19] Yet even in Marx the ultimate goal remains reconciliation, the restoration of unalienated Being through the abolition of class contradiction. The continuity with Hegel remains: pain is the passage to harmony, not its enduring condition.

Nietzsche overturns this teleology by affirming pain as intrinsic to life's creativity. In *The Gay Science* and *Thus Spoke Zarathustra*, suffering becomes the sign of vitality, the means through which life exceeds itself.[20] The will to power affirms tension as necessity. However, Nietzsche's physiological metaphors prevent this affirmation from attaining systematic ontological form. Pain remains existential, not structural. Freud inherits Nietzsche's insight but internalizes it. The psyche is organized around repression and conflict; pleasure and pain are not opposites but phases of a single economy of excitation.[21] Psychoanalysis thereby anticipates the thesis advanced here: the self is produced through resistance. Yet Freud's metapsychology retains an implicitly mechanistic model of energy that prevents the leap from psychology to ontology.

Phenomenology and existentialism bring pain to the threshold of ontology. Husserl describes the body as the zero point of orientation, the source of affective self-givenness.[22] Heidegger radicalizes this insight by identifying mood (*Befindlichkeit*) as the way in which Being is disclosed.[23] Anxiety (*Angst*) reveals the nothing that

---

[19] Karl Marx, *Economic and Philosophic Manuscripts of 1844*, trans. Martin Milligan (Moscow: Progress, 1959).

[20] Friedrich Nietzsche, *The Gay Science*, trans. Walter Kaufmann (New York: Random House, 1974); *Thus Spoke Zarathustra*, trans. R. J. Hollingdale (Harmondsworth: Penguin, 1961).

[21] Sigmund Freud, *Beyond the Pleasure Principle*, trans. James Strachey (New York: Norton, 1961).

[22] Edmund Husserl, *Ideas Pertaining to a Pure Phenomenology and to a Phenomenological Philosophy*, trans. F. Kersten (The Hague: Nijhoff, 1982).

[23] Martin Heidegger, *Being and Time*, trans. John Macquarrie and Edward Robinson (New York: Harper, 1962), § 40.

underlies all beings. Nevertheless, for Heidegger, anxiety is a disclosure rather than a structure; it reveals Being but is not itself constitutive of it. Sartre's and Merleau-Ponty's analyses of the body as situation and ambiguity continue the same tendency.[24] They describe the experience of limitation but stop short of granting limitation ontological primacy. Pain remains an existential condition of human life, not a feature of Being as such.

The emergence of process philosophy and critical realism in the twentieth century provides the conceptual tools to overcome this residual anthropocentrism. Whitehead's *Process and Reality* defines reality as a series of occasions of experience whose essence is relational feeling.[25] Discord, not harmony, is the motor of concrescence. Every actual entity is the unification of conflicting data; negative prehension is as essential as positive. In Roy Bhaskar's *Dialectic: The Pulse of Freedom*, this principle is re-articulated in explicitly realist terms. Reality consists of stratified mechanisms that persist through transformation, and transformation presupposes resistance.[26] Bhaskar's concept of the pulse of freedom describes the rhythmic transition between constraint and agency that constitutes Being's dynamism. Pain is the phenomenological side of this rhythm, the feeling of resistance through which freedom becomes intelligible.

In retrospect, the absence of pain from metaphysical first principles appears not as oversight but as systematic repression. Classical ontology's identification of Being with perfection, Christian theology's transcendental consolation, Enlightenment rationalism's dream of mastery, and dialectical philosophy's teleology of reconciliation all express the same refusal: the refusal to accept resistance as intrinsic. The ontology of pain seeks to rectify this

---

[24] Maurice Merleau-Ponty, *Phenomenology of Perception*, trans. Donald A. Landes (London: Routledge, 2012).
[25] A. N. Whitehead, *Process and Reality*, 22–40.
[26] Roy Bhaskar, *Dialectic: The Pulse of Freedom*, 18–27.

refusal by placing tension, rather than harmony, at the foundation of the real.

To treat pain as ontological requires a method capable of bridging the empirical and the metaphysical without collapsing one into the other. Pure phenomenology risks reducing ontology to experience; pure realism risks abstracting experience out of existence. The approach taken in this work, therefore, is a synthesis of critical realism, dialectical method, and phenomenological description. It assumes, first, that reality is independent of thought; second, that it is internally differentiated and processual; and third, that experience is one of the ways in which reality becomes self-revealing. In this sense, philosophy does not stand outside the world it describes. Thought is a mode of Being's reflexivity.

Critical realism provides the scaffolding for such an approach. Bhaskar's ontological stratification—distinguishing the real, the actual, and the empirical—offers a framework within which pain can be situated.[27] The empirical corresponds to the domain of experienced events, the actual to events whether or not they are experienced, and the real to the causal structures that generate them. Pain, though empirical in its manifestation, belongs to the real insofar as it indicates the operation of resistance within a self-organizing system. Its phenomenological immediacy reveals a causal structure: the system's relation to its own limitation. This insight allows pain to be analyzed both as subjective feeling and as ontological event.

The dialectical method translates this ontological insight into conceptual movement. If Being is self-differentiating activity, then contradiction and resistance are not logical errors but ontological necessities.[28] Every system sustains itself by integrating opposition; without resistance there would be no identity. Pain is the affective registration of that integration process. The dialectic, properly

[27] Roy Bhaskar, *A Realist Theory of Science* (Brighton: Harvester, 1975), 56–60.
[28] Ibid.; see also Bhaskar, *Dialectic: The Pulse of Freedom*, 4–7.

understood, is therefore not a speculative procedure but a description of how reality endures through tension. To suffer pain is to participate in the dialectic of Being.

Phenomenology complements this realist dialectic by specifying how resistance appears in experience. Husserl's analysis of bodily awareness as the zero-point of orientation demonstrates that affect precedes cognition.[29] Merleau-Ponty develops this insight into a general theory of embodiment: perception is the body's negotiation of its own finitude.[30] Pain is the limit-term of this negotiation, the experience of the world's refusal to yield entirely to intention. Phenomenology thereby furnishes the vocabulary through which ontology can be made experientially intelligible.

The integration of these methods yields what may be termed *reflexive realism*: a philosophical position that treats Being as both independent and self-revealing. Reflexivity, in this context, is not merely cognitive but structural. A process is reflexive when it incorporates feedback from its operations into its continuation. In physical systems this feedback manifests as self-regulation; in biological systems as adaptation; in psychological systems as consciousness. Pain, as the felt registration of feedback failure, appears at every level of complexity. It signals the cost of persistence. In this way, pain becomes the universal marker of reflexivity.

To clarify this claim, several core terms must be defined with precision.

Being refers to the total field of existence understood as self-organizing activity. It is neither substance nor pure becoming but a structured process that maintains identity through transformation.[31]

29 Edmund Husserl, *Ideas Pertaining to a Pure Phenomenology*, 65–70.
30 Maurice Merleau-Ponty, *Phenomenology of Perception*, 91–105.
31 Bhaskar, *Dialectic: The Pulse of Freedom*, 132–145.

Whitehead's term "creativity" captures this dynamic essence: Being is the production of relations.[32]

Reflexivity designates the capacity of a process to internalize the effects of its actions and adjust accordingly. It is the ontological principle underlying feedback and consciousness alike. Reflexivity is not restricted to mental phenomena; it is intrinsic to any system that persists through time. The brain, the organism, the ecosystem, and the cosmos all exhibit forms of reflexivity proportional to their complexity.[33]

Pain names the experiential form of reflexivity under constraint. It is the awareness of limitation as such. Neuroscience confirms that pain is not a simple sensory event but an integrative process involving multiple cortical and subcortical regions.[34] The anterior cingulate cortex, insula, and prefrontal cortex interact to produce the experience of unpleasantness, anticipation, and meaning.[35] This distributed organization suggests that pain functions as a higher-order monitoring system: it evaluates the system's own state. In ontological terms, this means that pain is reflexivity encountering its boundary. Where reflexivity fails, pain intensifies; where it adapts, pain becomes knowledge.

Constraint refers to the relational structure that enables form. In systems theory, constraint is not merely limitation but organization. Stuart Kauffman and Ilya Prigogine have shown that self-organization arises precisely where energy flow meets constraint.[36]

---

[32] Whitehead, *Process and Reality*, 21–23.

[33] Francisco Varela, Evan Thompson, and Eleanor Rosch, *The Embodied Mind: Cognitive Science and Human Experience* (Cambridge, MA: MIT Press, 1991), 44–47.

[34] Antonio Damasio, *Descartes' Error: Emotion, Reason, and the Human Brain* (New York: Putnam, 1994), 141–154.

[35] Irene Tracey and Patrick D. Wall, "Pain and the Brain: From Nociception to Cognition," *Journal of Neurology, Neurosurgery & Psychiatry* 75, no. 10 (2004): 1366–1371

[36] Stuart A. Kauffman, *The Origins of Order: Self-Organization and Selection in Evolution* (New York: Oxford University Press, 1993), 25–28; Ilya Prigogine and Isabelle

Thermodynamic gradients create the conditions for structure, and living systems maintain themselves by exploiting these gradients. Pain, as the experiential analogue of constraint, is the affective recognition of this thermodynamic law. It is the subjective side of entropy management.

Freedom is the capacity to act within constraint rather than the power to transcend it. Bhaskar defines freedom as "the recognition and transformation of necessity."[37] From this perspective, pain is the first recognition of necessity, the signal that transformation is required. Freedom begins not in choice but in awareness of limitation. The will arises when reflexivity learns to integrate its pain into purposeful adaptation. The organism that recoils learns avoidance; the mind that reflects learns freedom.

These definitions yield a coherent metaphysical schema. Being is self-organizing activity; reflexivity is its mode; constraint is its condition; pain is its affective form; freedom is its emergent function. This schema permits a unified interpretation of phenomena across scales. The pain of an organism, the crisis of a civilization, and the instability of an ecosystem all express the same underlying process: the effort of Being to sustain itself through resistance.

The methodological consequence is that ontology must become interdisciplinary without ceasing to be philosophical. Scientific theories of self-organization, feedback, and adaptation provide empirical correlates of the structures described here. Yet philosophy remains necessary because these structures are not self-interpreting. The sciences describe the mechanisms of persistence; philosophy elucidates their meaning. An ontology of pain restores meaning to mechanism without mystification. It shows that what science

---

Stengers, *Order Out of Chaos: Man's New Dialogue with Nature* (New York: Bantam, 1984).

[37] Bhaskar, *Dialectic: The Pulse of Freedom*, 128.

describes as error or stress is, in phenomenological terms, the universe's mode of learning itself.

The distinction between pain as structure and suffering as condition must be maintained. Pain, in this framework, is ontological and unavoidable; suffering is historical and contingent. Suffering arises when the reflexive capacity of a system is obstructed, when pain cannot be integrated into adaptation. This distinction clarifies the ethical implications of the theory: the task is not to abolish pain but to transform suffering by expanding reflexivity. Moral and political progress are measured not by the quantity of pain reduced but by the depth of awareness achieved through it.

Finally, the methodological unity of the project can be summarized in the following proposition: ontology and epistemology are reciprocally reflexive. To know pain is already to participate in the structure it describes. The philosopher who thinks pain reproduces, in cognition, the same dynamic that sustains reality in Being. Pain is thus both the object and the method of this inquiry. It grounds a mode of thought adequate to the world's own self-reflective process.

The twentieth century left philosophy divided between analytic and continental traditions, both of which failed, though for different reasons, to account for pain as ontological. Analytic metaphysics, grounded in logical positivism and later in modal realism, construed Being as a set of possible states rather than a field of resistance. The emphasis on language and formal logic, from Frege and Russell to Quine and Kripke, removed affect from the domain of ontology altogether.[38] Continental thought, in turn, inherited phenomenology's focus on experience but often reduced ontology to the horizon of meaning. Both traditions, despite their opposition, presuppose a representational gap between subject and world. Pain, as the immediate and unmediated registration of constraint, resists

---

[38] W. V. O. Quine, *From a Logical Point of View* (Cambridge, MA: Harvard University Press, 1953).

representation; hence both traditions render it philosophically invisible.

The analytic tendency is exemplified by the dispositional essentialism of contemporary metaphysics, in which reality consists of causal powers whose manifestation conditions are logically specified.[39] This model accounts for potentiality but not for resistance. Pain, however, is precisely the experience of potentiality encountering resistance. It is the moment when a causal power fails to manifest smoothly, revealing the tension that analytic formalism abstracts away. To integrate pain into ontology is therefore to expose the affective basis of causal necessity: the fact that existence is not merely structured but strained.

Continental philosophy, while sensitive to the phenomenology of strain, often dissolves it into discourse. Structuralism and post-structuralism, by construing subjectivity as a linguistic effect, transformed pain into a function of representation. For Foucault, suffering is the by-product of disciplinary regimes that inscribe power on the body.[40] For Derrida, the wound is textual, the trace of différance within signification.[41] Deleuze and Guattari, in rejecting both transcendence and representation, came closest to recovering the ontological dimension of pain, describing the body without organs as a plane of intensities that is both productive and painful.[42] Yet even here, the metaphysical implications remain underdeveloped; intensity is affirmed, but its necessary resistance is not fully conceptualized.

---

[39] Stephen Mumford, *Dispositions* (Oxford: Oxford University Press, 1998).
[40] Michel Foucault, *Discipline and Punish: The Birth of the Prison*, trans. Alan Sheridan (New York: Pantheon, 1977).
[41] Jacques Derrida, *Writing and Difference*, trans. Alan Bass (Chicago: University of Chicago Press, 1978).
[42] Gilles Deleuze and Félix Guattari, *A Thousand Plateaus: Capitalism and Schizophrenia*, trans. Brian Massumi (Minneapolis: University of Minnesota Press, 1987).

THE ONTOLOGICAL PRIMACY OF PAIN

The so-called "affective turn" in contemporary theory, represented by thinkers such as Brian Massumi and Eve Kosofsky Sedgwick, restores affect to theoretical prominence but often detaches it from ontology.[43] Affect becomes a pre-personal force without structure, a spontaneity rather than a constraint. The ontology of pain advanced here reverses this emphasis. Pain is not a free intensity but a structured resistance; it is affect disciplined by form. Where affect theory celebrates fluidity, the ontology of pain restores the dignity of limit. Limit is not the negation of becoming but its condition.

Recent movements in speculative realism and new materialism share this impulse to return to ontology but remain ambivalent about the role of resistance. Quentin Meillassoux's *After Finitude* demands a philosophy that affirms the absolute independence of the real, yet his notion of contingency as the only necessity abstracts the real from any internal differentiation.[44] Graham Harman's object-oriented ontology restores the autonomy of things but conceives relation only as withdrawal, not as tension.[45] Byung-Chul Han, in contrast, diagnoses contemporary culture as the disappearance of negativity, the exhaustion produced by positivity without resistance.[46] Han's sociological phenomenology of fatigue resonates closely with the present project, for both identify the anaesthesia of modern life as a metaphysical symptom: the repression of pain leads to the collapse of reflexivity.

To situate pain ontologically is therefore to provide what contemporary philosophy has lacked — a theory of *necessary resistance*. Every structure, whether physical, biological, or social, persists

---

[43] Brian Massumi, *Parables for the Virtual: Movement, Affect, Sensation* (Durham, NC: Duke University Press, 2002); Eve Kosofsky Sedgwick, *Touching Feeling: Affect, Pedagogy, Performativity* (Durham, NC: Duke University Press, 2003).
[44] Quentin Meillassoux, *After Finitude: An Essay on the Necessity of Contingency*, trans. Ray Brassier (London: Continuum, 2008).
[45] Graham Harman, *The Quadruple Object* (Alresford: Zero Books, 2011).
[46] Byung-Chul Han, *The Burnout Society*, trans. Erik Butler (Stanford, CA: Stanford University Press, 2015).

through constraint. In thermodynamics, this is expressed as entropy; in evolution, as adaptation; in society, as alienation. The ontology of pain unifies these domains under a single principle: Being learns itself through resistance. This unification does not erase empirical difference but provides a metaphysical grammar within which difference can be understood.

The epistemological consequence of this ontology is a reconception of knowledge as endurance. If Being is reflexive tension, then knowing is the capacity to sustain contradiction without collapse. Truth is not correspondence between statement and fact but the resilience of thought under pressure. Error is the necessary condition of learning; pain is its sign. This conception aligns with the model of predictive processing in contemporary neuroscience, which describes the brain as a system for minimizing prediction error.[47] In phenomenological terms, prediction error is pain: the affective signal of discrepancy between expectation and reality. Knowledge, both biological and philosophical, is the iterative integration of such signals.

Ethically, this ontology rejects both hedonism and asceticism. If pain is structural, its elimination is neither possible nor desirable. The moral task is to cultivate reflexivity, to transform pain into awareness. Compassion thus becomes a mode of cognition: to recognize the pain of another is to perceive the shared structure of constraint that constitutes all being. Violence, conversely, is ontological denial — the refusal to acknowledge interdependence and the projection of resistance outward. This understanding converges with Simone Weil's notion that attention to suffering is the highest form of justice, for it aligns the individual will with the

---

[47] Karl Friston, "The Free-Energy Principle: A Unified Brain Theory?," *Nature Reviews Neuroscience* 11 (2010): 127–138.

structure of reality.[48] Ethics, in this view, is the art of remaining in contact with Being's own friction.

Politically, the ontology of pain exposes the metaphysical basis of domination. Modern institutions — the market, the state, the corporation — function as systems of pain distribution. They convert ontological resistance into social hierarchy. Capital translates the pain of labour into the abstraction of value; the state translates vulnerability into security and coercion. These mechanisms stabilize existence by externalizing pain, yet in doing so they conceal its source. The crises of modernity — economic inequality, ecological degradation, and psychic exhaustion — are not aberrations but revelations. They are moments when concealed pain reasserts itself. To politicize pain is not to sentimentalize it but to render visible the ontological structure of power. A just society would not promise to eliminate suffering but to render the process of endurance transparent and shared.

Epistemologically, this realism implies a new form of philosophical practice. If pain is the medium of reflexivity, philosophy itself must be a practice of endurance. The concept cannot claim immunity from resistance; thought must include its own difficulty as content. The ideal of total clarity that guided both analytic precision and phenomenological intuition must yield to a dialectical patience. Knowledge is achieved not by transcending pain but by thinking through it. The method of this book, therefore, is itself performative: its difficulty mirrors the resistance it describes.

The integration of this ontology into contemporary discourse has further implications for environmental and planetary thought. Ecological crisis represents the point at which the global system encounters the limits of its self-forgetting. The exploitation of nature is metaphysically identical to the repression of pain: both are denials

---

[48] Simone Weil, *Gravity and Grace*, trans. Emma Craufurd (London: Routledge, 2002), 72.

of resistance. To recognize the planet as a reflexive system — one that learns through breakdown — is to extend ontology beyond the human without abandoning the affective dimension. The Earth, in its climate feedbacks and evolutionary adaptations, exhibits the same structure of endurance that defines Being. Ecological awareness, therefore, is ontological compassion at the planetary scale.

Finally, this ontology culminates in a philosophical spirituality that redefines the sacred as transparency. To live spiritually is not to escape pain but to perceive in it the activity of Being itself. Conscious suffering becomes participation in the world's self-knowledge. As Weil observed, "to suffer is to feel the distance between what is and what should be; to accept this distance is to touch the real."[49] The reflexive acceptance of pain transforms endurance into understanding. The sacred, thus conceived, is the act of worlding itself — the process by which Being perceives Being.

The chapters that follow develop these implications systematically. Chapter 1 establishes pain as the medium of Being's self-relation. Chapter 2 analyses freedom as emergent reflexivity under constraint. Chapters 3 and 4 examine how social institutions distribute and abstract pain. Chapter 5 interprets modernity as the metaphysical refusal of limitation. Chapter 6 extends the argument to the planetary scale, and Chapter 7 culminates in a conception of philosophical spirituality grounded in the transparency of reflexivity. Together, these analyses constitute an ontology of pain as the foundation of metaphysics, ethics, and political thought.

To think pain is to think the real without evasion. Pain marks the point where thought meets its own limit and learns to continue. Philosophy begins and ends there

[49] Ibid., 98.

CHAPTER I

The Ontology of Pain: Being as Reflexivity

1. The First Sensation

A philosophy of Being begins from an event that reveals existence to itself. For classical metaphysics, this event was creation. For phenomenology, it was appearance. For existentialism, it was consciousness. The present work begins from a different event: resistance. Before there is thought, there is pressure. Before there is cognition, there is contact. Pain is the first form of contact through which existence becomes aware of its own finitude.

Pain is the earliest and most universal relation. It marks the moment when Being, in striving to continue, encounters what resists it. This encounter is not external to life but identical with it. An organism exists by virtue of what it can endure. Endurance is not an incidental property but the grammar of Being. The degree to which something exists is the degree to which it can persist under resistance. The organism that ceases to resist ceases to exist.

Pain therefore is not opposed to life but identical with it. Life is the capacity to register resistance and to transform that registration into adaptation, memory, and structure. Where there is no resistance, there is no perception, no difference, no growth. Total comfort would be indistinguishable from Non-Being. Pain is the affective sign of reality. To feel pain is to be in contact with what exists. To exist is to be subject to pain.

In this sense, pain is the first cognition. It is not merely sensation but a primitive form of knowledge. The organism that feels pain learns the shape of its own boundary. The feeling of pressure contains the first distinction between inside and outside, self and other. This distinction is not yet conceptual, but it is real. The touch that hurts marks the border that thinks.

The history of Being, considered as process, is the history of this first sensation unfolding into structure. From the molecular resistance that stabilizes matter to the evolutionary struggle that stabilizes life, existence is a continual translation of resistance into organization. In thermodynamic terms, pain corresponds to the work required to maintain order against entropy.[50] Every system pays for its persistence by transforming external pressure into internal form. This cost is the ontological meaning of pain.

The tendency of metaphysics has been to interpret order as harmony and disorder as suffering. Yet order itself is the product of constraint. The crystalline lattice forms only through limitation of movement; the living cell maintains its identity by regulating exchange. In both cases, the experience of constraint is inseparable from the achievement of form. The very possibility of Being depends upon the capacity to feel and manage resistance. Pain is the internal registration of that necessity.

This is evident even in the simplest organisms. The withdrawal reflex of a unicellular creature is not an accident of biology but the expression of an ontological law: to persist, a system must detect and respond to what resists it. Without this detection there can be no feedback, no adaptation, no continuation. The earliest nervous systems evolved precisely to mediate this process of registration and response.[51] Pain, in its most elementary form, is the signal through which Being feels the cost of its own persistence.

To feel pain, therefore, is to participate in the first gesture of existence. Every cry, every contraction, every recoil is a recapitulation of the original act by which Being becomes aware of its boundary. The pressure that hurts is the same pressure that

---

[50] Ludwig Boltzmann, *Lectures on Gas Theory*, trans. Stephen G. Brush (Berkeley: University of California Press, 1964), 32–35.

[51] Antonio Damasio, *The Strange Order of Things: Life, Feeling, and the Making of Cultures* (New York: Pantheon, 2018), 19–22.

defines. In this way, pain is not an imperfection within existence but the proof that existence is self-differentiating. The stone fractures, the organism flinches, the mind despairs; all express the same law. Being learns itself through resistance.

The smoothness imagined by metaphysical idealism would entail the absence of this law. It would be a state without boundary or difference, in which nothing could appear or know itself. Pain is the refusal of such void. It is the self's acknowledgement of the otherness through which it subsists. Even in physics, where energy and matter are conceived in impersonal terms, resistance is the necessary correlate of work. To act without friction would be to act without reality. The same applies to thought. To think without tension would be to think nothing.

Pain is thus the most elementary structure of awareness. It is through pain that Being attains to the first form of knowledge: the recognition that it is not alone. Resistance introduces relation, and relation introduces form. Ontology begins there. Before the categories of substance and attribute, before the dualities of subject and object, there is the fact of contact felt as pain. From that contact all differentiation arises.

2. Being as Reflexivity

If pain is the first sensation, reflexivity is the first structure. Pain does not merely happen to Being; it folds Being back upon itself. The moment of pain divides what is into two moments: the one who feels and the feeling that is felt. This division constitutes the first interiority. Reflexivity arises when existence encounters itself as resistance and responds.

To speak of reflexivity is to reject the notion of Being as inert substrate. Being is not a substance that receives experiences; it is activity that becomes aware of itself through its own interruptions. The fold by which Being touches itself and recognizes the touch as its own is the origin of consciousness. What is felt as pain is not an alien intrusion into Being but Being sensing its own limit.

This conception modifies the classical metaphysical distinction between matter and mind. If matter is understood as passive extension and mind as active reflection, then pain reveals their common ground. Reflection arises from resistance. The act of self-awareness is not an ethereal capacity added to matter but the necessary consequence of the friction internal to Being. To think is to fold. To feel pain is to experience that fold as resistance. Consciousness, in this view, is not external to matter but matter become reflexive through pain.

The development of consciousness follows this structure. The nervous system does not invent feeling but refines the capacity of Being to register itself. Each level of complexity introduces new forms of feedback and hence new modes of reflexivity. The reflex arc of the spinal cord, the affective circuitry of the limbic system, and the reflective processes of the neocortex are successive deepening of the same ontological pattern. Consciousness is an evolutionary elaboration of reflexivity under constraint.[52] Pain is the signal that sustains this elaboration. Where there is no capacity for pain, there is no adaptive awareness.

In phenomenological terms, pain is not one sensation among others but the condition of all sensation. Every perception involves resistance. The feel of texture, the perception of weight, and the effort of thought each contain an element of tension. Husserl describes this as the passive synthesis of affectivity, the background tonality that constitutes the sense of presence.[53] Without affective resistance, the world would not appear as world. Pain is the zero degree of that resistance, the limit at which synthesis threatens to

---

[52] Antonio Damasio, *Self Comes to Mind: Constructing the Conscious Brain* (New York: Pantheon, 2010), 102–108.
[53] Edmund Husserl, *Ideas Pertaining to a Pure Phenomenology and to a Phenomenological Philosophy*, 64–70.

collapse. It is the edge where the continuity of experience confronts the real.

Critical realism interprets the same structure causally. For Bhaskar, reality is differentiated and layered; mechanisms operate within constraints that define their powers.[54] Reflexivity arises when a mechanism becomes aware of its own constraint and acts upon it. This process is not merely epistemic but ontological. Being itself learns. Pain is the point at which such learning becomes felt, the empirical trace of ontology's self-modification. The transition from mechanism to agency is thus the transition from unregistered resistance to conscious endurance.

Process philosophy reaches a similar conclusion through different means. In Whitehead's cosmology, every actual entity prehends others and integrates them into a new unity. The prehension of discord produces what he calls negative emotion, an experience of incompatibility that must be resolved through creative advance.[55] This is the metaphysical prototype of pain. The world, in each of its occasions, suffers its own tensions into new order. Creativity is not spontaneous emergence but the transformation of suffering into form.

Pain, then, is not a defect within Being but the principle of its continuity. It keeps reflexivity open. When Being moves without resistance, it ceases to learn; it becomes static. When resistance is encountered, reflexivity deepens; awareness intensifies. The same dynamic operates in the life of the mind. Thought develops only through contradiction. The philosopher who never suffers doubt learns nothing. The interruption of certainty is the condition of truth. In this sense, pain is epistemological as well as ontological. It

---

[54] Roy Bhaskar, *A Realist Theory of Science* (Brighton: Harvester, 1975), 56–60.
[55] A. N. Whitehead, *Process and Reality: An Essay in Cosmology*, corrected ed. (New York: Free Press, 1978), 40–44.

is the experience of the limit that thought must incorporate to advance.

Reflexivity therefore defines Being as a loop rather than a line. Every act of existence involves a return upon itself. The loop is not closed; it is open and dynamic. It sustains itself through feedback, correction, and renewal. Pain is the tension that holds this loop together. It prevents Being from dissolving into undifferentiated flow. The structure of pain is the structure of persistence. It is the internal necessity that gives form to freedom.

At the level of the human, this reflexivity acquires self-consciousness. The experience of "I suffer" is the articulation of Being's ontological grammar in personal form. Yet even here the structure remains the same. The self is a process, not a substance; its identity arises from the ongoing integration of resistance. The narratives of selfhood, the moral distinctions of good and evil, and the cultural practices of endurance are elaborations of the same fundamental loop. The ethical dimension of pain thus follows from its ontology. To endure consciously is to participate in the reflexive labour of Being itself.

Pain is the hinge that connects necessity to freedom. It marks the point where Being becomes capable of transformation without ceasing to be itself. Every system that can feel its constraint possesses the possibility of change. Reflexivity is the mechanism by which this possibility is realized. Through pain, Being recognizes that it is both limited and active. It does not simply endure the world; it learns through it. Pain is the first teacher. The philosopher's task is to make explicit what all life already enacts: the knowledge that Being is reflexive through suffering.

3. The Reflexive Structure of the Real

If pain is the affective form of reflexivity, then reflexivity itself must be understood as the structural principle of reality. To describe Being as reflexive is not to introduce consciousness into matter but to recognize that all persistence entails self-relation. A system that endures must register the effects of its own operations and integrate them into further activity. Reflexivity, in this sense, is the minimal condition for ontological stability. Pain is the experiential index of this condition in the domain of life and mind.

In the physical world, reflexivity appears as feedback between energy, form, and entropy. Thermodynamics teaches that every organized system maintains itself by countering the tendency toward disorder. Entropy measures the degree of unavailable energy; order represents the local reduction of entropy through work.[56] This work is always performed against resistance. A structure exists only insofar as it expends energy to sustain itself. The cost of that expenditure, experienced internally in living systems, is pain. The relation between energy and constraint that defines the physical world reappears within experience as the relation between effort and suffering. The equivalence is not metaphorical but structural.

The second law of thermodynamics, often interpreted as the guarantee of decay, is also the principle of learning. Systems that maintain themselves far from equilibrium do so by using feedback to detect and respond to perturbations.[57] They survive by converting resistance into information. This is true of chemical networks, ecosystems, and social institutions alike. Reflexivity is the law by which such systems adapt. Pain is the phenomenological registration of that same law. It marks the point at which the maintenance of form requires reorganisation.

In information theory, feedback and error correction play a similar role. A system processes information by comparing expected signals with received ones and adjusting accordingly. The difference between expectation and reality generates what Claude Shannon

---

[56] Ludwig Boltzmann, *Lectures on Gas Theory*, 32–38.

[57] Ilya Prigogine and Isabelle Stengers, *Order Out of Chaos: Man's New Dialogue with Nature* (New York: Bantam, 1984), 169–171.

called information, a measure of surprise.[58] The brain operates according to this same logic, minimizing prediction error through continuous updating.[59] Pain corresponds to high prediction error, the felt awareness that the world is not conforming to the model. To learn is to transform pain into coherence. The predictive brain is therefore a physical instantiation of Being's general reflexive pattern. It reproduces, at the level of cognition, what the cosmos performs at every scale.

The continuity between physics, biology, and mind is not a speculative analogy but an ontological necessity. Each domain manifests the same triadic relation of energy, constraint, and adaptation. In physical terms, the interaction of force and resistance yields structure. In biological terms, the interaction of organism and environment yields life. In mental terms, the interaction of expectation and experience yields consciousness. Pain is the invariant that links these levels. It is the form in which resistance becomes registered as information. Wherever systems learn, they feel. The universe, understood reflexively, is an economy of feeling through which Being clarifies itself.

This does not imply that the cosmos is conscious in any anthropomorphic sense. It means that consciousness, where it arises, expresses an ontological tendency already latent in matter. The structure of feedback that governs thought is a refinement of the structure that governs energy flow. Reflexivity is the deep form of reality's self-organization. Pain is its affective aspect, appearing in organisms as the cost of sustained complexity. The human nervous system does not introduce pain into the world; it makes explicit what the world already enacts implicitly.

---

[58] Claude E. Shannon, "A Mathematical Theory of Communication," *Bell System Technical Journal* 27, no. 3 (1948): 379–423.
[59] Karl Friston, "The Free-Energy Principle: A Unified Brain Theory?," *Nature Reviews Neuroscience* 11 (2010): 127–138.

Whitehead's process ontology anticipates this interpretation. Every actual entity, he writes, is "a throbbing unity of many feelings."[60] The phrase captures both the dynamism and the tension of reality. The throbbing is not metaphorical but structural: Being pulsates between integration and disintegration. This pulse is the source of novelty. Pain, in this view, is the rhythm of existence felt from within. It is the alternating contraction and release through which the universe sustains itself in time. Bhaskar's dialectical realism extends the same principle to the social and historical domain. The pulse of freedom is the rhythmic mediation of constraint and transformation, an ontological heartbeat that underlies all becoming.[61] Both thinkers, in different registers, describe reflexivity as the metabolism of Being.

Modern systems theory confirms that this metabolism is universal. Maturana and Varela's concept of autopoiesis defines life as a network that produces and maintains itself through recursive processes.[62] Each component participates in generating the network that produces it. Pain, interpreted ontologically, is the affective correlate of this recursion. It is the feeling of self-maintenance, the local awareness of the cost of systemic coherence. To exist autopoietically is to experience resistance. Pain is therefore not a contingent feature of some beings but the essential sign of Being as such.

From this perspective, the dualism of matter and mind dissolves into a continuum of reflexive processes differentiated by degree, not by kind. The simplest feedback loop and the most complex self-reflective consciousness share the same structural logic. What differentiates them is not their ontological nature but their capacity to register and integrate resistance. Pain is the measure of this capacity. Where reflexivity is limited, pain is pure sensation; where it

---

[60] A. N. Whitehead, *Process and Reality*, 28.
[61] Roy Bhaskar, *Dialectic: The Pulse of Freedom* (London: Verso, 1993), 18–25.
[62] Humberto R. Maturana and Francisco J. Varela, *Autopoiesis and Cognition: The Realization of the Living* (Dordrecht: Reidel, 1980), 78–82.

is developed, pain becomes understanding. In both cases, it is the same phenomenon observed at different levels of self-reference.

This continuity implies that the study of pain offers a privileged access to the structure of reality itself. Pain is not merely a topic for psychology or ethics but a clue to ontology. To analyse pain is to analyse the mechanism by which Being sustains itself. The task of philosophy, then, is not to transcend pain but to think it fully — to understand how the real becomes conscious through its own resistance. Pain is the hinge between physics and phenomenology, between necessity and freedom. It reveals that the universe is not inert but recursive, that the real is not a static given but a dynamic process of self-learning.

The reflexive structure of the real thus unifies ontology, epistemology, and ethics. Being is reflexive; knowledge is the reflexivity of being known; goodness is the reflexivity of being endured consciously. Pain binds these dimensions together. It is the sign that reality is not indifferent but participatory, that existence knows itself through feeling. The cosmos is a field of suffering and learning, a self-sensing process that generates awareness through tension. To exist is to participate in this process, to carry within one's own experience the pulse of Being's reflexivity.

4. The Ontological Function of Pain

Having established that reflexivity is the fundamental structure of Being and that pain is its affective form, it remains to articulate the ontological function of pain. Pain is not merely the subjective correlate of resistance; it is the mechanism through which Being acquires knowledge of itself. To say that Being is reflexive is to say that it contains within itself the capacity for self-modification. Pain is the mode in which that capacity becomes operative. It converts resistance into information and information into transformation.

Every organized system is defined by the feedback loops that enable it to maintain coherence in the face of perturbation. In living systems, these loops are affective as well as mechanical. Pain functions as a corrective signal that interrupts homeostasis, indicating that the system's equilibrium has been disturbed.[63] The interruption compels reorganisation. The physiological reaction to injury, the emotional reaction to loss, and the intellectual reaction to contradiction are all expressions of the same logic. Pain announces that a limit has been reached and demands that it be reconfigured. Through this function, pain transforms necessity into learning.

The adaptive role of pain in biology demonstrates the universality of this mechanism. Organisms incapable of experiencing pain are unable to avoid harm or to adjust to environmental change.[64] Pain is therefore not a maladaptive defect but the precondition for adaptation. Evolutionary processes favour systems that can feel resistance because feeling resistance enables modification. The same principle applies beyond biology. Thought evolves by recognizing error, societies evolve by enduring crisis, and the cosmos evolves by transforming tension into new forms of order. Pain is the functional constant across these scales.

To understand pain as ontological cognition is to recognize that knowing is not a neutral act but an affective event. The emergence of awareness from sensation depends upon the ability to sustain dissonance without immediate resolution. Pain provides the temporal duration required for such integration. In the absence of pain, stimuli would be registered and extinguished instantaneously, leaving no trace for reflection. Pain slows experience, forcing the system to attend. In this sense, pain introduces time into being. It stretches immediacy into process. The delay between impact and adaptation constitutes the interval in which consciousness arises. Pain, therefore, is the temporal form of reflexivity.

---

[63] Joseph LeDoux, *The Emotional Brain: The Mysterious Underpinnings of Emotional Life* (New York: Simon & Schuster, 1996), 138–142.
[64] S. J. Cox et al., "Congenital Insensitivity to Pain: Clinical and Genetic Analysis of a Large Family," *Brain* 129, no. 3 (2006): 573–581.

In phenomenological terms, this means that awareness is inseparable from effort. The intentional arc that Merleau-Ponty describes as the structure of perception presupposes tension between body and world.[65] The act of reaching, seeing, or understanding is always a negotiation of distance. Pain is the registration of that negotiation when distance resists closure. It is the mark of finitude within the structure of intentionality. Every perception carries within it the residue of this resistance, a remainder of pain that cannot be eliminated without abolishing relation itself. The subject exists only because the world resists its grasp.

At the ontological level, pain ensures that Being remains open to novelty. Resistance prevents closure; it guarantees that no system can fully coincide with itself. Pain interrupts the tendency toward totalization that characterizes both life and thought. It is the safeguard of freedom within necessity. Without pain, systems would lapse into inertia; with pain, they are compelled to transform. Pain thus plays the same role in metaphysics that contradiction plays in logic: it is the source of movement. The dialectic of pain and adaptation underlies all becoming.

Critical realism provides the conceptual vocabulary for this insight. Bhaskar distinguishes between the intransitive dimension of Being, which exists independently of knowledge, and the transitive dimension, which consists of the human practices through which Being is known.[66] Pain belongs to both dimensions simultaneously. As the registration of constraint, it is intransitive, part of the structure of the real. As awareness of that constraint, it is transitive, part of the process of knowing. Pain mediates the two by converting ontological tension into epistemic content. It is the bridge between Being and knowledge. Through pain, the real becomes conscious of itself.

---

[65] Maurice Merleau-Ponty, *Phenomenology of Perception* (London: Routledge, 2012), 95–102.

[66] Roy Bhaskar, *The Possibility of Naturalism* (Brighton: Harvester, 1979), 23–25.

The same principle appears in Hegel's notion of *Erfahrung* or experience as the movement of consciousness through its own contradictions.[67] Every stage of the *Phenomenology* begins with certainty and ends in the suffering of refutation. This suffering is productive; it transforms knowledge. What Hegel describes dialectically, the ontology of pain describes affectively. Experience is the endurance of contradiction. Pain is the felt form of *Erfahrung*. It is the negativity through which spirit realizes itself in the finite.

The ontological function of pain can now be formulated in general terms. Pain is the medium of reflexive transition. It performs three interconnected tasks: revelation, integration, and transformation. It reveals the existence of resistance, integrates that resistance into awareness, and transforms awareness into new form. These tasks correspond to the three moments of dialectical movement: negation, mediation, and sublation. In each case, pain is the motor. It is the experience of negation, the effort of mediation, and the energy of transformation. Without pain, Being would be static, knowledge would be inert, and freedom would be impossible.

This functional analysis also clarifies the ethical significance of pain. Because pain mediates between Being and awareness, it cannot be treated as morally negative in itself. The moral value of pain depends on the degree of reflexivity it enables. Pain that leads to awareness is educative; pain that overwhelms reflexivity is destructive. The task of ethics is therefore not to abolish pain but to create conditions in which it can be integrated. Compassion, in this framework, is the recognition that all beings share the labour of reflexivity. To acknowledge another's suffering is to perceive one's participation in the same ontological process.

---

[67] G. W. F. Hegel, *Phenomenology of Spirit*, trans. A. V. Miller (Oxford: Oxford University Press, 1977), 55–60.

In the social domain, this principle translates into a theory of history. Civilisations endure and transform through collective experiences of resistance. Economic crisis, political upheaval, and cultural disintegration are the macrocosmic equivalents of pain. They are moments when established forms encounter their limits. The persistence of history depends upon such moments. Each epoch learns through the friction of its own contradictions. Pain is the pedagogy of Being.

Finally, the ontological function of pain has implications for the understanding of meaning. Meaning arises where resistance is endured and integrated. The act of interpretation is itself a form of adaptation, a reorganization of the self in response to what resists comprehension. Pain thus grounds not only knowledge but value. To suffer is to be compelled to signify. The arts, religions, and sciences of humanity are successive attempts to translate pain into understanding. Every symbol is the fossil of an endured resistance. Being, through humanity, writes its pain into language.

5. The Dialectic of Pain and Order

Pain, as the previous section established, is the medium through which Being encounters its limits and transforms itself. The persistence of this process across all levels of reality implies that pain and order are dialectically inseparable. Order is not the negation of pain but its provisional resolution. Pain generates form, and form in turn conceals the memory of pain. Every stable structure is the crystallized remainder of an earlier tension. When the tension that produced it returns, the form dissolves and a new order emerges. The dialectic of pain and order therefore constitutes the fundamental rhythm of existence.

In physical systems, this dialectic manifests as the relation between energy, entropy, and equilibrium. Energy flows produce organization only through resistance. Prigogine's theory of dissipative structures shows that systems far from equilibrium maintain their order by consuming entropy, transforming disorder into new configurations of stability.[68] This continuous self-ordering depends upon internal friction. Without resistance, energy would dissipate into uniformity; without flow, resistance would congeal into stasis. The tension between these two tendencies sustains the world's dynamic coherence. Pain, in living systems, is the experiential registration of this universal tension. It is the affective echo of entropy management, the subjective face of the universe's thermodynamic dialectic.

At the biological level, this dialectic produces evolution. Organisms develop through cycles of adaptation and breakdown. Pain signals maladaptation, compelling mutation or behavioural change. The evolutionary record is a chronicle of resisted forms. Every new function arises from the failure of a previous one. Pain ensures that failure becomes instruction. In the absence of pain, selection would have no internal criterion. The continuity of life across geological time depends on this capacity to feel and respond to resistance. The same process repeats in individual development. Growth, both physical and psychological, requires the integration of pain. Muscular strength results from microtrauma and repair; emotional maturity arises from loss endured and transformed. The capacity for order depends upon the capacity for suffering.

In cognitive systems, the dialectic of pain and order governs learning. Predictive processing models describe the brain as a hierarchy of predictions that aim to minimize error between expectation and perception.[69] Pain corresponds to prediction error that cannot be immediately resolved. It compels reorganization of the model, yielding more accurate representations. Each new equilibrium of understanding is therefore the result of a preceding disequilibrium. Pain functions as the epistemic motor of cognition. The mind's

---

[68] Ilya Prigogine and Isabelle Stengers, *Order Out of Chaos: Man's New Dialogue with Nature* (New York: Bantam, 1984), 170–175.

[69] Karl Friston, "The Free-Energy Principle: A Unified Brain Theory?," *Nature Reviews Neuroscience* 11 (2010): 127–138.

order, like the body's, is the product of tension endured and integrated.

The same dialectic governs social and historical processes. Societies stabilize themselves by institutionalizing the distribution of pain. Economic systems allocate effort and reward; political systems distribute vulnerability and protection. These arrangements crystallize the memory of collective suffering into durable forms of order. Marx's analysis of alienation reveals this mechanism with particular clarity. Labour, as painful exertion, externalizes human activity into objects and institutions that confront their creators as alien powers.[70] Capital, in this sense, is reified pain, the accumulation of labour's endurance. Yet this reification is unstable. When the concealed suffering of the productive base exceeds its threshold, crisis ensues. Revolution is the social form of pain's return. The dialectic of pain and order thus explains both the persistence and the periodic breakdown of historical structures. What Hegel called the cunning of reason is, at the material level, the cunning of pain.

In the ethical domain, this dialectic expresses the relation between endurance and transcendence. Moral systems arise from the effort to give meaning to pain. The commandments, virtues, and prohibitions of ethical life codify strategies of endurance that proved viable under historical conditions. When those conditions change, the moral order begins to fail. Pain reappears as guilt, despair, or revolt, demanding new forms of value. The moral progress of humanity is therefore a series of integrations of suffering. Each ethical breakthrough universalizes the recognition of pain. The abolition of slavery, the extension of rights, and the invention of welfare institutions are not merely political events but ontological movements. They enlarge the reflexive capacity of the species. The measure of moral advancement is the degree to which pain becomes consciously shared.

---

[70] Karl Marx, *Economic and Philosophic Manuscripts of 1844*, trans. Martin Milligan (Moscow: Progress, 1959), 72–76.

At the planetary scale, the dialectic of pain and order manifests as ecological crisis. Industrial civilization has sought to externalize pain completely by transforming human labour into mechanical energy and environmental cost. The apparent triumph of comfort has produced systemic instability. Climate disruption is the planetary return of repressed resistance. The Earth, as a self-regulating system, reacts to human activity as any organism reacts to injury: through feedback that restores equilibrium at a higher level of tension.[71] The suffering of the biosphere is not merely a moral challenge but a metaphysical event. It is Being reasserting its law of reflexivity against the illusion of limitless expansion. Pain, once again, functions as correction.

The dialectic of pain and order thus describes the logic of existence across all domains. The world endures through tension, and every effort to abolish tension results in collapse. Equilibrium is always temporary, a pause in the ongoing conversion of suffering into structure. The philosophical consequence is that harmony cannot be the ultimate aim of Being. The ideal of perfect order is metaphysically incoherent, for it would require the absence of resistance and thus the cessation of existence itself. The true telos of Being is not rest but reflexivity, not peace but participation in the endless transformation of pain into form.

From this follows a redefinition of metaphysical terms. Substance is not that which persists unchanged but that which sustains change through endurance. Form is the memory of pain successfully integrated. Freedom is the capacity to participate consciously in the dialectic of pain and order. Evil, by contrast, is the attempt to deny or externalize pain, to maintain order by suppressing its origin. Such denial produces opacity, the loss of reflexivity that characterizes both tyranny and ignorance. The good is whatever increases transparency,

---

[71] James Lovelock, *Gaia: A New Look at Life on Earth* (Oxford: Oxford University Press, 1979), 89–94.

enabling pain to be recognized as the medium of Being's self-relation.

In this framework, the metaphysical question of theodicy is transformed. The problem is not why suffering exists in a world created by the good, but why order exists in a world that endures through resistance. Suffering is not the anomaly; it is the principle. The emergence of structure, meaning, and life are the continuous transmutations of suffering into stability. The world is good not because it is painless but because it can learn through pain. To affirm Being is therefore to affirm the dialectic of pain and order as the source of all reality.

6. The Teleology of Being

The dialectic of pain and order implies a direction, not toward final harmony but toward increasing reflexivity. If pain is the medium through which Being learns itself, then the history of Being can be interpreted as a progressive clarification of this self-knowledge. The world does not evolve toward rest but toward transparency. Every form of existence, from the atom to the organism to the consciousness that reflects on them, participates in this teleology of awareness. The goal of Being is not perfection but lucidity.

Teleology has long been treated with suspicion, particularly since the rise of mechanistic science. The assumption that the universe aims at ends appeared anthropomorphic, a remnant of premodern cosmology. Yet the rejection of teleology often confuses purpose with pattern. To say that Being has direction is not to claim that it possesses intention. It is to recognize that self-organizing systems display tendencies that are neither random nor externally imposed. Reflexivity constitutes such a tendency. Every process that sustains itself must, over time, improve its sensitivity to resistance. The increase of reflexivity is therefore not accidental but structural.[72]

The unfolding of reflexivity follows a rhythm of tension and release. Each new level of organization arises when previous constraints are integrated into higher forms of feedback. In physical systems, this manifests as the emergence of stable attractors that regulate energy flow. In biological systems, it appears as the evolution of complex nervous networks capable of internal representation. In social systems, it becomes the development of language, morality, and science. At every level, pain initiates this progression by marking the point where existing structures fail. The failure becomes the site of learning. The teleology of Being thus proceeds through crisis. The world advances by feeling its own inadequacy.

This movement can be described as the gradual reduction of opacity. Opacity refers to the inability of a system to perceive the causes of its own conditions. When opacity prevails, pain appears meaningless. The animal feels injury as arbitrary, the human suffers injustice as absurd. Reflexivity transforms opacity into intelligibility by linking pain to its cause. To understand pain is to reduce opacity. The history of consciousness can be read as the progressive internalization of causality. Science, philosophy, and art are different modes of this internalization. They transform suffering into comprehension, thereby expanding the field of awareness in which Being knows itself.[73]

The culmination of this process would be pure transparency, a state in which all resistance is consciously recognized as intrinsic to Being. Such transparency would not abolish pain but would integrate it completely. Pain would persist as feeling but not as alienation. The distinction between suffering and understanding would collapse. In

---

[72] Terrence W. Deacon, *Incomplete Nature: How Mind Emerged from Matter* (New York: W. W. Norton, 2012), 205–210.

[73] Hans Jonas, *The Phenomenon of Life: Toward a Philosophical Biology* (Evanston, IL: Northwestern University Press, 1966), 127–132.

theological language, this corresponds to the idea of redemption; in metaphysical terms, to the full reflexivity of the real. Yet complete transparency may be an asymptotic ideal rather than an achievable state. The condition of existence is finitude, and finitude implies residual opacity. What can be attained is not the end of pain but its conscious participation in the process of being.

Whitehead's concept of concrescence offers a useful analogue. Each actual occasion, he writes, aims at satisfaction, the integration of discordant data into harmony.[74] This satisfaction is never absolute; it gives rise to new contrasts in subsequent occasions. The universe, therefore, is an endless sequence of partial integrations. Pain accompanies each phase as the felt resistance of integration. The teleology of Being is thus iterative rather than final. Its goal is not completion but the ongoing transformation of opacity into transparency.

In Bhaskar's dialectical ontology, a similar idea appears as the process of "ontological depth."[75] Reality consists of stratified levels, each emerging from the contradictions of the previous. Freedom expands as systems become aware of their causal conditions. This awareness does not abolish necessity but recognizes it as internal to agency. The same relation governs the metaphysical teleology of pain. As Being becomes aware of its own constraints, it transforms them into conditions of freedom. Pain, when reflexively understood, is no longer mere suffering but participation in the self-determination of the real.

From this follows a new definition of freedom. Freedom is not the absence of constraint but the transparent relation to it. The individual or society that denies pain remains enslaved by it; the one that understands pain becomes autonomous. To be free is to know the necessity that structures one's being and to act in conscious relation to it. The philosophical and political implications of this

---

[74] A. N. Whitehead, *Process and Reality: An Essay in Cosmology*, 43–46.
[75] Roy Bhaskar, *Dialectic: The Pulse of Freedom* (London: Verso, 1993), 130–134.

definition are profound. It transforms liberation from a project of escape into a project of comprehension. Freedom is reflexivity applied to existence. The ontology of pain thus grounds a realist conception of emancipation. The path to liberation lies not in the refusal of suffering but in its integration into awareness.[76]

The teleology of Being culminates, therefore, in a form of philosophical spirituality. If pain is the medium through which Being becomes self-aware, then to endure pain consciously is to participate in the reflexive process of the universe itself. Spiritual experience, in this sense, is the intensification of reflexivity to the point where the boundary between individual and world becomes transparent. The mystic who perceives unity through suffering does not transcend the world but experiences its ontological structure directly. Compassion, similarly, is the recognition that the same reflexive process operates in all beings. To attend to the pain of another is to witness Being learning itself through them. The ethical and the metaphysical coincide.

In conclusion, the teleology of Being is the gradual self-illumination of reality through pain. The cosmos, understood in this light, is a self-reflective process that advances toward awareness through resistance. Every atom, organism, and mind participates in this labor. The purpose of philosophy is not to deny this labor but to comprehend it. To think pain is to think Being in its truth. Pain is the world's way of perceiving itself. The transparency toward which Being moves is not the erasure of pain but its complete understanding. When that understanding deepens, existence becomes more lucid, and lucidity itself becomes the highest form of being.

---

[76] Ibid., 137–140.

CHAPTER II

Emergent Free Will: Constraint as the Condition of Agency

1. The Recursive Structure of Freedom

The problem of free will has endured as the central riddle of philosophy because it appears to divide Being against itself. If the universe is governed by causality, freedom seems impossible; if freedom exists, causality appears incomplete. Both conclusions are unsatisfactory, for each reduces one pole of reality to the other. The deterministic view denies the experiential fact of agency, while the libertarian view suspends agency in metaphysical isolation. The persistence of this paradox indicates that freedom, like pain, has been misconstrued as an exception rather than as a property intrinsic to Being.

Freedom is not a rupture in causality but an emergent mode of it. To understand how freedom arises, we must first grasp how Being itself operates reflexively. As established in the ontology of pain, existence is not inert but self-relating; every system persists through feedback with its own limits. Reflexivity therefore constitutes the ground of agency. A system that can sense and respond to resistance already exhibits the minimal condition of freedom. The capacity for freedom is identical to the capacity for learning through constraint.[77]

This perspective reframes the metaphysical problem. The traditional opposition between determinism and freedom presupposes a linear model of causation in which events succeed one another in external sequence. Yet the structure of Being, as revealed by pain, is recursive rather than linear. Causality is circular and hierarchical; every act is both the product and the modifier of its own conditions. The recursive loop, not the chain, is the basic unit of reality.[78] Within such a loop, freedom appears not as the negation of causality but as

---

[77] Roy Bhaskar, *Dialectic: The Pulse of Freedom* (London: Verso, 1993), 4–7.
[78] Francisco Varela, Evan Thompson, and Eleanor Rosch, *The Embodied Mind: Cognitive Science and Human Experience* (Cambridge, MA: MIT Press, 1991), 44–47.

its reflexive moment. The agent is free not because it escapes determination but because it internalizes it. Constraint becomes the medium of choice.

Systems theory provides an empirical analogue to this conception. An autopoietic system, as Maturana and Varela define it, maintains itself by recursively producing the components that constitute it.[79] Its operations are circular: output becomes input, effect becomes cause. Agency in such a system consists not in external intervention but in internal modulation. The organism cannot step outside its conditions, yet within them it can vary its responses, generating novelty through self-reference. Freedom, in this framework, is the capacity of a system to use constraint as information. The more refined the system's reflexivity, the greater its freedom.

Pain plays a central role in this recursive process. It marks the moment when the system's model of itself conflicts with its actual state. The organism that feels pain becomes aware of a discrepancy between intention and reality. This awareness forces adaptation. The recursive processing of pain thus becomes the foundation of agency. Every act of freedom is preceded by the feeling of constraint. To act freely is to respond intelligently to the necessity that resists one's will. Freedom is the conversion of resistance into purpose.[80]

This interpretation aligns with contemporary models of predictive processing in neuroscience. The brain, according to Friston's free energy principle, minimizes the difference between predicted and actual sensory input by updating its internal models.[81] The experience of error, or prediction failure, generates affective signals that guide learning. Pain is the affective signature of high prediction error, the felt tension between the organism's expectations and the

---

[79] Humberto Maturana and Francisco J. Varela, *Autopoiesis and Cognition: The Realization of the Living* (Dordrecht: Reidel, 1980), 78–82.
[80] Antonio Damasio, *The Strange Order of Things: Life, Feeling, and the Making of Cultures* (New York: Pantheon, 2018), 45–50.
[81] Karl Friston, "The Free-Energy Principle: A Unified Brain Theory?," *Nature Reviews Neuroscience* 11 (2010): 127–138.

world's feedback. Agency emerges as the capacity to modulate this error rather than to eliminate it. The organism achieves freedom by transforming uncertainty into structure. Thus, the neurocomputational process of prediction error minimization is the physiological expression of the metaphysical dialectic between pain and freedom.

The recursive nature of freedom also resolves the long-standing opposition between necessity and contingency. Determinism, in its classical form, treats necessity as external compulsion. In contrast, a reflexive ontology treats necessity as internal relation. To say that an agent acts necessarily is to say that it acts according to the structure that defines its being. Freedom does not require the suspension of necessity but its recognition. When the system knows its own limits, necessity becomes self-expression. Constraint ceases to appear as foreign and becomes the medium of transformation. This internalization of necessity constitutes the essence of emergent freedom.[82]

Freedom therefore exists on a continuum with reflexivity. At its most basic, freedom is the capacity of matter to sustain variation under constraint. At higher levels, it becomes the self-conscious ability of mind to reinterpret necessity as meaning. Pain mediates this ascent. Each time Being feels resistance, it opens a new possibility of integration. Freedom is not given; it is learned through pain. The history of freedom, both biological and cultural, is the history of resistance made intelligible. From the first movements of matter to the deliberations of thought, Being discovers its freedom by enduring the necessity that defines it.

This conception has profound implications for metaphysics. It abolishes the dualism between mechanical and mental causation that has haunted philosophy since Descartes. Both are expressions of the same recursive structure. What distinguishes the human from the

---

[82] Roy Bhaskar, *A Realist Theory of Science* (Brighton: Harvester, 1975), 58–62.

physical is not exemption from causality but the depth of reflexivity. The human can experience constraint as meaning, whereas the physical can only enact it as law. Yet the law and the meaning are structurally continuous. They represent different articulations of the same ontological logic: the conversion of resistance into coherence.[83]

The recursive model of freedom also clarifies the moral significance of pain. If freedom emerges through the reflexive integration of constraint, then the capacity to endure pain consciously becomes the measure of moral maturity. The ethical task is not to abolish necessity but to comprehend it. The one who refuses pain remains bound by it; the one who integrates it acts freely. Freedom thus coincides with understanding. To know what constrains one is to act within it intelligently. The wise person, in this framework, is not the one who suffers least but the one who understands suffering most completely. Pain, endured reflectively, becomes the substance of freedom itself.

2. Constraint as the Ontological Condition of Agency

The philosophical tradition has treated constraint as the negation of freedom. To be free, in the classical sense, was to act without external compulsion. From Aristotle's distinction between voluntary and involuntary motion to Kant's conception of autonomy as obedience to a law one gives oneself, freedom has been defined by contrast with determination.[84] Yet this opposition presupposes an image of Being as inert substance and of causality as linear force. Once Being is understood as reflexive process rather than static substance, the relation between constraint and agency must be rethought. Constraint becomes not the negation of freedom but its enabling condition.

---

[83] Terrence W. Deacon, *Incomplete Nature: How Mind Emerged from Matter* (New York: W. W. Norton, 2012), 250–255.

[84] Immanuel Kant, *Groundwork for the Metaphysics of Morals*, trans. Mary Gregor (Cambridge: Cambridge University Press, 1998), 44–47.

In a reflexive ontology, constraint is synonymous with form. A system exists only insofar as it limits its own possibilities. The cell persists because its membrane constrains the flow of matter and energy; the mind endures because the nervous system restricts and organizes sensory input. Constraint defines identity by establishing boundaries of operation. Without such boundaries, there could be no differentiation, and without differentiation, no action. The apparent limitation is thus the foundation of agency. To act is to act within form. The more structured the form, the more complex the possibilities of action it allows.[85]

This logic extends beyond biology. In physics, constraint appears as the conservation laws that govern the transformation of energy. These laws do not impede motion but make motion possible by establishing the parameters within which it can occur. The same holds for social and cognitive systems. Language, for example, is a structure of constraints that enables communication. Every grammatical rule that forbids certain combinations simultaneously opens the possibility of meaning. Freedom without rule is noise; rule without freedom is silence. The interplay between the two constitutes intelligibility. Constraint, therefore, is the grammar of freedom.

From the perspective of critical realism, this relation between constraint and freedom reflects a deeper ontological principle. Bhaskar's notion of the "pulse of freedom" designates the movement through which necessity becomes the condition of agency.[86] Freedom, in this sense, is not the absence of causal structure but its transformation into self-determination. A mechanism becomes an agent when it recognizes its own constraint and acts in accordance with it. Pain, as the affective awareness of constraint, is the means through which this recognition occurs.

---

[85] Francisco Varela, *Principles of Biological Autonomy* (New York: Elsevier, 1979), 55–59.

[86] Roy Bhaskar, *Dialectic: The Pulse of Freedom* (London: Verso, 1993), 18–25.

Through pain, the system becomes conscious of the limits that define its being. To integrate this consciousness is to achieve agency. The structure of freedom is thus dialectical: necessity gives rise to its own transcendence through self-recognition.

The notion that constraint is constitutive of agency is supported by the science of self-organization. Complex systems exhibit emergent behaviour precisely because they are constrained. The interactions among their components generate higher-order regularities that cannot be reduced to individual parts. Terrence Deacon has shown that such emergent order arises from "constitutive absence," the way constraints on physical processes give rise to new causal properties.[87] What is absent or restricted becomes the ground of new possibilities. The living organism, for instance, does not merely resist entropy but uses it as the precondition of vitality. The same logic governs consciousness. Thought arises from the constraints imposed by the body and the environment. Agency is the expression of limitation internalized as structure.

Pain plays a decisive role in this dynamic. It marks the point at which constraint becomes felt. In physiological terms, pain is the signal of stress on the system's boundaries; in psychological terms, it is the experience of frustrated intention. Both signify the encounter between form and force, between what is desired and what is possible. The intensity of pain corresponds to the degree of dissonance between these two orders. Yet this dissonance is also the source of learning. The organism or mind that can endure and integrate such tension expands its domain of reflexivity. Constraint becomes information, and information becomes agency. The recursive transformation of pain into awareness is the ontological mechanism of freedom.[88]

---

[87] Terrence W. Deacon, *Incomplete Nature: How Mind Emerged from Matter* (New York: W. W. Norton, 2012), 203–211.

[88] Antonio Damasio, *The Feeling of What Happens: Body and Emotion in the Making of Consciousness* (New York: Harcourt Brace, 1999), 153–158.

The interdependence of constraint and agency is evident in the organization of the nervous system. The brain operates through inhibitory as well as excitatory processes. Inhibition, far from suppressing action, allows for selective attention and intentional control. Freedom of thought arises from the capacity to withhold response, to sustain contradiction without immediate resolution. Pain functions as the signal that initiates this inhibition. It arrests automatic reaction and creates the reflective interval necessary for choice. Without constraint there would be no deliberation; without inhibition there would be no will. Constraint thus constitutes the temporal condition of freedom.[89]

From the standpoint of metaphysics, this insight implies that the very structure of reality is volitional in potential. Every system that contains internal constraint also contains the possibility of agency. The difference between mechanical and volitional behaviour is not ontological but reflexive. The machine reacts; the organism acts; the conscious being deliberates. Each stage represents a deeper internalization of constraint. The emergence of freedom is therefore the deepening of reflexivity through the awareness of limitation. In this sense, pain is the evolutionary signal of the universe learning to will. The feeling of being constrained is the birth of self-direction.

Freedom, thus understood, is inseparable from finitude. To be finite is to be bounded, and to be bounded is to possess form. Infinite Being would lack the differentiation necessary for action. Finitude provides the condition under which freedom becomes meaningful. The will is not free in spite of its limits but because of them. The human struggle against necessity is the process through which necessity becomes conscious of itself. The moral and spiritual significance of this truth cannot be overstated. The cultivation of freedom requires the cultivation of sensitivity to constraint. A

[89] Michael S. Gazzaniga, *Who's in Charge? Free Will and the Science of the Brain* (New York: Ecco, 2011), 104–108.

civilization that seeks only to abolish limits thereby undermines the basis of agency itself. In denying pain, it abolishes the medium of growth.

This ontology of freedom therefore demands a reorientation of ethics and politics. If constraint is the ground of agency, then justice cannot be conceived as the elimination of limitation but as the equitable distribution of meaningful constraint. The problem of modernity, in this light, is not that it imposes too many limits but that it distributes them unevenly and conceals their ontological necessity. Some are burdened with pain while others are shielded from it; the result is alienation on both sides. The ethical task is to reveal the shared structure of constraint that underlies all forms of existence. Only in recognizing pain as universal can freedom be genuinely collective.[90]

In summary, constraint is not the antithesis of agency but its condition. Pain, as the affective registration of constraint, functions as the mediator between necessity and freedom. Every act of will is a reconfiguration of limitation. The more reflexively a system can integrate its constraints, the freer it becomes. Freedom is therefore not an escape from determination but the conscious participation in determination's unfolding. It is the art of using necessity as material for self-expression.

3. The Phenomenology of Volition

The phenomenology of volition reveals how the abstract ontological relation between constraint and freedom becomes lived experience. To will is not to transcend causality but to feel it from within. Every act of choice arises as a moment of tension between impulse and inhibition, between desire and resistance. This tension is not accidental; it constitutes the very form of consciousness. The

[90] Simone Weil, *Gravity and Grace*, trans. Emma Craufurd (London: Routledge, 2002), 78–80.

experience of volition is the experience of constraint becoming internal and reflexive.

Husserl described intentionality as the defining structure of consciousness, the directedness of thought toward something other than itself.[91] Yet intentionality, by its nature, involves friction. The object of intention resists complete assimilation by the subject. This resistance is the seed of volition. The will arises as the affective registration of the gap between intention and fulfilment. Pain, in this context, is the feeling of intentionality's incompleteness. It signals the persistence of alterity within experience. Volition begins when this pain is not merely suffered but used — when the subject converts resistance into direction. To will is to respond to the world's resistance with structure.

Merleau-Ponty's phenomenology of the body clarifies this further. He argues that the lived body is not an object among others but the medium of access to the world.[92] Movement and perception are expressions of the same embodied intentionality. Pain disrupts this continuity, revealing the body as both subject and object. When one feels pain, the body appears as other to itself; it resists the will's command. Yet this interruption is precisely what makes self-awareness possible. The body's resistance to its own movement generates the reflective distance in which volition becomes conscious. The experience of willing thus contains within it the same structure as the experience of pain: Being encountering itself as limit.

Neuroscientific evidence corroborates this phenomenological insight. The initiation of voluntary action involves a temporal sequence in which motor readiness precedes conscious decision.[93] Benjamin Libet's experiments showed that brain activity signalling

---

[91] Edmund Husserl, *Ideas Pertaining to a Pure Phenomenology and to a Phenomenological Philosophy*, trans. F. Kersten (The Hague: Nijhoff, 1982), 80–83.
[92] Maurice Merleau-Ponty, *Phenomenology of Perception*, trans. Donald A. Landes (London: Routledge, 2012), 90–96
[93] Benjamin Libet et al., "Time of Conscious Intention to Act in Relation to Onset of Cerebral Activity," *Brain* 106, no. 3 (1983): 623–642.

movement begins milliseconds before subjects report choosing to act. While often interpreted as evidence against free will, this finding instead supports the recursive model of volition. The conscious experience of willing is a higher-order integration of multiple feedback loops within the brain. The sense of agency arises when these loops converge into a coherent self-model. Pain, again, serves as a modulatory signal within this process. It anchors the abstract circuits of readiness in the concrete immediacy of the body. The will is not an immaterial entity but a hierarchical reflexivity distributed across neural, bodily, and environmental constraints.

Antonio Damasio's account of homeostasis provides the biological foundation for this view. Organisms act to maintain internal balance in the face of perturbation. When deviation from equilibrium occurs, affective signals emerge to guide correction.[94] The simplest form of such affect is pain. At higher levels, these signals become emotions and, eventually, deliberate decisions. The continuity between homeostatic regulation and conscious choice indicates that volition is a refinement of the same adaptive mechanism. Free will is homeostasis made reflective. The feeling of effort that accompanies choice is the lived trace of this regulatory process. The organism experiences its own activity as strain, and this strain becomes the substance of decision.

From an ontological perspective, the phenomenology of volition can be understood as the translation of Being's reflexivity into temporal form. When Being encounters resistance, it generates delay. This delay creates the interval in which awareness arises. Time, in this sense, is the internal rhythm of reflexivity. To choose is to occupy the interval between impulse and action, to inhabit the space where Being negotiates its own constraint. Pain, as the sensation of this delay, is the experiential correlate of freedom's emergence. It is not an obstacle to decision but its condition. Every act of will is preceded

---

[94] Antonio Damasio, *The Feeling of What Happens: Body and Emotion in the Making of Consciousness* (New York: Harcourt Brace, 1999), 141–144.

by a moment of friction that compels reflection. Freedom without friction would be instantaneous and therefore unconscious.

This understanding reconciles the apparent opposition between determinism and experience. Determinism describes the continuity of causal structure; phenomenology describes its internal articulation. The act of will is determined in its conditions but indeterminate in its integration. The system cannot choose its constraints, but it can choose how to relate to them. This relational freedom constitutes the essence of agency. The phenomenology of volition reveals this structure in lived form. When one feels the weight of decision, one is not encountering the limit of freedom but participating in its unfolding. The struggle to decide is the reflexivity of Being felt within time.[95]

Pain therefore functions as the ontological constant in the experience of will. It binds the physical, affective, and cognitive dimensions of agency into a single process. The individual who experiences conflict, hesitation, or remorse is not failing to be free but realizing freedom at its deepest level. Such experiences are the phenomenological traces of reflexivity itself. Freedom is not the absence of difficulty but the capacity to dwell within it consciously. To will is to endure contradiction without disintegration.

The metaphysical implication is that volition, rather than being an anomaly in nature, expresses the world's general law of self-determination. The structure of choice mirrors the structure of Being. Both involve tension, feedback, and adaptation. The experience of freedom is the consciousness of this structure in motion. Pain is its signature. When one feels the effort of deciding, one feels Being thinking through the self. The personal will is a local intensification of the universal reflexivity of existence. To act freely

---

[95] Evan Thompson, *Mind in Life: Biology, Phenomenology, and the Sciences of Mind* (Cambridge, MA: Harvard University Press, 2007), 216–219.

is to participate knowingly in that reflexivity, to become a site through which Being transforms constraint into meaning.[96]

4. The Emergence of Moral Agency

If volition is the lived form of Being's reflexivity, moral agency is its social and evaluative extension. The moral dimension arises when the recursive process of awareness becomes intersubjective, when the self recognizes its freedom as implicated in the freedom of others. At this stage, the dialectic of pain and constraint acquires ethical meaning. The individual does not simply experience resistance as personal limitation but as part of a shared field of necessity. To act morally is to act in awareness of this shared reflexivity.

In its earliest anthropological forms, morality appears as codified responses to pain. Prohibitions against harm, ritual acts of atonement, and systems of reciprocity all originate in the recognition that suffering binds individuals to one another.[97] Pain functions here as a universal language of interdependence. Every moral law is an attempt to formalize the management of pain within a community. Yet these formalities are not merely social conventions; they reflect the ontological structure of Being itself. Just as constraint enables freedom within the individual, social constraint enables collective agency. Moral order transforms the chaos of competing wills into a higher-level reflexivity, where pain is distributed, regulated, and ideally transformed into justice.

This transformation depends on the internalization of constraint. The passage from obedience to autonomy, which Kant describes as the essence of moral maturity, is in ontological terms the passage from external to internal reflexivity.[98] The law ceases to appear as an

---

[96] Francisco Varela, Evan Thompson, and Eleanor Rosch, *The Embodied Mind: Cognitive Science and Human Experience* (Cambridge, MA: MIT Press, 1991), 215–220.
[97] René Girard, *Violence and the Sacred*, trans. Patrick Gregory (Baltimore: Johns Hopkins University Press, 1977), 8–12.
[98] Immanuel Kant, *Groundwork for the Metaphysics of Morals*, 54–59.

alien imposition and becomes recognized as the condition of one's own agency. The categorical imperative thus expresses a metaphysical truth: that freedom consists in acting according to the necessity one has consciously appropriated. To will the good is to will the structure that sustains freedom for all. Pain, in this framework, is both the test and the teacher of autonomy. The individual who resists temptation, endures injustice, or sacrifices comfort for principle participates in the reflexive labour of Being. Moral will is the ethical face of ontological reflexivity.

In phenomenological terms, this labour manifests as conscience. Conscience is the affective awareness of the self's participation in a shared field of constraint. It arises when one's actions generate dissonance within that field. The pang of guilt is pain transposed from the physical to the moral plane. It signals a disruption in reflexive equilibrium. Yet, as with all pain, this disruption has an educative function. Conscience compels the reorganization of volition, aligning personal desire with collective necessity. Moral development, like biological adaptation, proceeds through cycles of resistance and integration. The capacity to feel moral pain is therefore the measure of ethical reflexivity. To lack this capacity is to remain trapped in the immediacy of self-interest.[99]

The emergence of moral agency can also be traced through the evolution of social complexity. As human societies expanded beyond kinship groups, the direct reciprocity of personal relations was replaced by abstract systems of law and exchange. These systems redistributed pain by mediating conflict through symbolic means. Money, state, and institution functioned as externalized forms of conscience, translating the management of suffering into structures of order. Yet, as later chapters will explore, these structures tend to ossify. The pain that once generated them becomes concealed within them. When the distribution of pain grows opaque, morality

---

[99] Paul Ricoeur, *Fallible Man*, trans. Charles A. Kelbley (New York: Fordham University Press, 1986), 112–116.

degenerates into legality, and reflexivity collapses into reification. Moral agency, in such conditions, requires the recovery of awareness — the capacity to perceive in institutional constraint the trace of shared suffering.[100]

At the individual level, moral agency emerges when volition becomes oriented toward universality. The self recognizes that its freedom is sustained by the freedom of others and that every act either expands or diminishes the total field of reflexivity. This recognition transforms pain into compassion. Compassion is the feeling of shared ontology, the awareness that the suffering of another is not foreign but internal to the same process through which one exists. It is the emotional form of metaphysical insight. The moral agent acts not from external duty but from identification with the reflexive movement of Being itself. Ethical maturity therefore coincides with ontological transparency. To see clearly that all freedom is conditioned is to will in harmony with that conditioning. Moral law and metaphysical truth converge.[101]

This convergence can be clarified through Hegel's account of ethical life (*Sittlichkeit*). For Hegel, true freedom is realized not in abstract choice but in the rational institutions of family, civil society, and the state.[102] These structures embody the collective self-recognition of spirit. Yet the ontology of pain adds a critical inflection to this dialectic. If spirit externalizes itself in institutions, it also risks forgetting the suffering that gave rise to them. Ethical life becomes authentic only when those institutions retain their reflexivity, when they continue to mediate pain rather than conceal it. The collapse of moral order occurs when pain is repressed, when collective constraint ceases to be consciously shared. Restoration of moral

---

[100] Karl Marx, *Capital*, vol. 1 (London: Penguin, 1976), 129–133.
[101] Simone Weil, *Gravity and Grace* (London: Routledge, 2002), 89–92.
[102] G. W. F. Hegel, *Elements of the Philosophy of Right*, trans. H. B. Nisbet (Cambridge: Cambridge University Press, 1991), 220–225.

agency requires the reactivation of awareness within these forms. The good society is one that feels.

In psychological terms, this process corresponds to what Damasio calls the somatic marker hypothesis: emotions guide decision-making by encoding the body's history of pain and pleasure.[103] Moral reasoning, accordingly, depends upon affective memory. Rationality alone cannot ground ethical choice; it must be informed by the felt record of constraint. The moral agent is one who can endure and interpret these somatic signals at the highest level of abstraction. The unity of emotion and reflection in conscience exemplifies the same recursive pattern observed throughout nature: the conversion of pain into awareness. Ethics is the homeostatic regulation of freedom.

The metaphysical significance of moral agency thus extends beyond the human domain. It represents the point at which Being becomes capable of valuing its own reflexivity. Through moral awareness, the universe achieves a form of self-care. The moral act preserves the conditions of Being's continued learning. Evil, in contrast, is not merely the infliction of harm but the refusal of reflexivity, the denial of participation in the shared structure of pain. To act immorally is to sever the feedback loop through which Being knows itself. Morality, therefore, is ontology turned conscious of its consequences.[104]

In conclusion, moral agency emerges when the recursive structure of freedom extends into intersubjective awareness. The individual who recognizes the necessity of constraint for all beings embodies the highest form of reflexivity. Pain, transfigured into compassion, becomes the substance of moral will. The ethical life is not the elimination of suffering but the intelligent participation in its

---

103 Antonio Damasio, *Looking for Spinoza: Joy, Sorrow, and the Feeling Brain* (New York: Harcourt, 2003), 121–124.
104 Roy Bhaskar, *Dialectic: The Pulse of Freedom*, 230–235.

distribution. Through moral action, Being becomes transparent to itself as shared endurance. Freedom finds its truth in solidarity.

5. The Metaphysical Integration of Freedom

Having established that pain, constraint, and reflexivity constitute the ontological ground of volition and moral agency, we can now articulate the metaphysical integration of freedom. The emergence of freedom is not an accidental property of complex systems but the necessary outcome of Being's recursive structure. Freedom is the mode through which Being becomes transparent to itself as process. It is not opposed to necessity but is the conscious articulation of it. To act freely is to participate knowingly in the reflexive movement of existence.

In traditional metaphysics, freedom has been treated as a privilege of mind or spirit, a power that separates humanity from the rest of nature. Yet the ontology of pain reveals a different logic. Freedom is not a discontinuity within Being but its culmination. The same principle that governs the feedback of physical systems governs the deliberation of the will. Reflexivity, at its most elemental, is the capacity to register and respond to resistance. As Being internalizes this capacity, it ascends through successive layers of self-awareness. Physical feedback becomes biological adaptation, biological adaptation becomes conscious volition, and conscious volition becomes moral and spiritual participation in the universal process. Freedom is thus the metaphysical telos of reflexivity, the moment when Being recognizes its own power of transformation.[105]

The integration of freedom and necessity can be formalized through the concept of emergent causality. In a reflexive ontology, causation operates both upward and downward. Lower-level constraints generate higher-order patterns, and these patterns in turn modify

[105] Roy Bhaskar, *Dialectic: The Pulse of Freedom* (London: Verso, 1993), 290–296.

their underlying conditions.[106] This recursive loop allows for novelty without violation of law. Freedom, accordingly, is downward causation exercised by reflexive wholes upon their parts. The conscious mind does not break the laws of physics; it redirects them by reconfiguring constraints. The same neural processes that determine reflexes become, through self-reference, the medium of choice. Freedom is law made reflexive. Determinism and agency are not contradictory but nested within one another.

This structure explains why freedom and pain are inseparable. The possibility of freedom depends on the persistence of resistance. Without tension, reflexivity would collapse into inertia. Every act of will therefore presupposes an encounter with necessity. Pain is the mark of that encounter. To suffer is to be free in potential; to act despite suffering is to actualize freedom. In this sense, the metaphysical integration of freedom is the reconciliation of Being with its own limits. Existence does not transcend its boundaries but deepens them into meaning. Freedom is the self-knowledge of finitude.[107]

The moral dimension of this integration becomes clear when we consider that freedom without awareness degenerates into domination. To act without perceiving the structure of constraint is to repeat it unconsciously. Only the reflexive understanding of necessity transforms power into agency. This distinction mirrors the difference between violence and creation, between compulsion and choice. In both the individual and the collective, genuine freedom requires that the pain of existence be faced and understood. The attempt to escape or deny pain results in the externalization of suffering onto others. The ontology of freedom therefore demands

---

[106] Terrence W. Deacon, *Incomplete Nature: How Mind Emerged from Matter* (New York: W. W. Norton, 2012), 345–350.

[107] Maurice Merleau-Ponty, *The Visible and the Invisible*, trans. Alphonso Lingis (Evanston, IL: Northwestern University Press, 1968), 127–132.

an ethics of transparency: to act freely is to act in full awareness of the constraints that one's action redistributes.[108]

At the cosmological scale, this process reveals the unity of evolution, history, and consciousness. Each domain is a manifestation of Being's effort to integrate resistance into higher forms of coherence. Evolution is the reflexivity of matter learning to feel; history is the reflexivity of feeling learning to think; consciousness is the reflexivity of thought learning to will. Through these stages, Being transforms passive endurance into active participation. Pain becomes meaning, and meaning becomes freedom. The universe, viewed through this lens, is not a mechanism but a pedagogy. It teaches itself through constraint. Freedom is the lesson Being gives to itself through the experience of pain.[109]

This conception dissolves the dualisms that have divided philosophy. Mind and matter, freedom and necessity, subject and object, are not opposed substances but phases of a single reflexive process. Each polarity arises from the differentiation of Being and is reconciled through awareness. The dualities that structure thought are expressions of the same logic that structures existence. To think reflexively is to mirror the world's own reflexivity. The unity of metaphysics and consciousness follows necessarily. Thought is Being's self-interpretation. Freedom is thought enacted in time.[110]

The integration of freedom also clarifies the meaning of spirituality within a philosophical framework. If Being is engaged in a continuous process of self-learning through pain, then spiritual life is the conscious identification with that process. The mystic, the scientist, and the moral agent are united by a common task: to render constraint transparent to awareness. Spiritual insight is not escape from the world but participation in its reflexive deepening. The

---

[108] Simone Weil, *Oppression and Liberty* (London: Routledge, 1958), 100–104.
[109] Ilya Prigogine and Isabelle Stengers, *Order Out of Chaos* (New York: Bantam, 1984), 172–178.
[110] Alfred North Whitehead, *Process and Reality*, 98–103.

sacred, therefore, is not transcendent but immanent. It is the act of reality perceiving itself. Pain, in this context, becomes revelation. To endure consciously is to assist Being in its own self-comprehension. Freedom is sanctified endurance.[111]

This metaphysical system resolves the ancient tension between the tragic and the rational views of existence. The tragic tradition, from Aeschylus to Nietzsche, saw pain as the ineradicable core of reality. The rational tradition sought to explain or overcome it. The ontology of pain integrates both: it accepts suffering as essential while revealing its cognitive function. Pain is not meaningless tragedy but the grammar of becoming. Freedom is its articulation into significance. The universe is neither absurd nor benevolent; it is intelligible through endurance.[112]

In this light, the moral and political crises of modernity acquire ontological significance. The alienation produced by industrial and digital abstraction is not merely economic but metaphysical. Humanity's technological power has outpaced its reflexivity. The global systems that now govern life externalize constraint to such a degree that pain becomes invisible. This invisibility undermines freedom by severing awareness from causation. The restoration of freedom in the contemporary world therefore requires the restoration of feeling. Philosophy's task is to reintroduce metaphysical consciousness into the management of material systems. The future of freedom depends on the recovery of pain as knowledge.[113]

Finally, the integration of freedom culminates in a new definition of the good. The good is whatever increases reflexivity, whatever

---

[111] Hans Jonas, *The Phenomenon of Life: Toward a Philosophical Biology* (Evanston, IL: Northwestern University Press, 1966), 180–183.
[112] Friedrich Nietzsche, *The Birth of Tragedy*, trans. Walter Kaufmann (New York: Vintage, 1967), 22–26.
[113] Karl Marx, *Economic and Philosophic Manuscripts of 1844*, 72–77.

enables Being to recognize itself through its constraints. Evil is whatever reduces reflexivity, whatever conceals or externalizes pain. The criterion of value is not pleasure or utility but transparency. To act well is to act in such a way that the loop of Being remains open. Pain endured consciously becomes wisdom; constraint understood becomes freedom. Through this process, Being achieves its ultimate purpose: to know itself without remainder. The metaphysical integration of freedom is thus the perfection of reflexivity, the moment when pain and knowledge become one.

CHAPTER III

The Social Ontology of Pain Distribution

1. The Materialization of Reflexivity

The passage from ontology to society marks not a transition between distinct domains but a transformation of the same structure into a new scale of operation. The reflexivity that defines Being at the metaphysical level manifests, at the social level, as collective organization. Society is the externalization of Being's self-relation. What in the individual is consciousness, in the collective becomes institution. Both are systems that endure through the management of resistance. The social world is therefore not an addition to nature but its amplification, an intensified loop of reflexivity distributed across many bodies.[114]

The origin of society is not in contract or calculation but in shared endurance. Before language or law, before the first division of labour, there existed the fact of collective vulnerability. Pain was the first bond. The experience of suffering together preceded all forms of exchange or governance. To endure collectively required coordination; coordination required structure. From this necessity emerged the earliest forms of order. The tribe, the ritual, the tool, and the rule are all secondary articulations of the same event: Being preserving itself through shared resistance.[115] The social is the metaphysical response of life to the pressure of existence.

Institutions, in this light, are not arbitrary inventions but crystallized reflexes. They materialize patterns of response to recurring forms of collective pain. The family mediates the pain of reproduction and loss; the market mediates the pain of scarcity; the state mediates the pain of conflict. Each arises from a need to stabilize what is otherwise unbearable. In doing so, they externalize the reflexivity

---

[114] Roy Bhaskar, *Dialectic: The Pulse of Freedom* (London: Verso, 1993), 178–182.
[115] Hans Jonas, *The Phenomenon of Life: Toward a Philosophical Biology* (Evanston, IL: Northwestern University Press, 1966), 87–90.

that once resided within individual awareness. Where the mind learns through the feedback of sensation, the institution learns through the feedback of history. The difference is one of scale, not of kind. Social systems, like biological ones, persist by integrating resistance into new forms of order.[116]

This structural homology between mind and society has often been intuited but rarely grounded ontologically. Durkheim's concept of collective consciousness, Marx's theory of social metabolism, and Parsons's systems model each capture aspects of it, yet all presuppose a metaphysical foundation they cannot fully articulate. The ontology of pain provides that foundation. If Being knows itself through resistance, then social order is Being's collective act of self-regulation. Pain, rather than pleasure, is the true social glue. The celebration of pleasure as the bond of society is historically recent and philosophically superficial. It mistakes the symptom of stability for its cause. Pleasure is the release of tension; society exists to manage tension. Pain is the principle of coherence.[117]

The division of labour illustrates this principle in concrete form. Labour divides because endurance divides. Each individual can bear only a portion of the total resistance required to sustain the collective. The specialization of functions is therefore the distribution of pain. The economy is a system for allocating endurance. Wages and professions quantify and regulate who suffers, when, and how much. The apparent neutrality of work conceals this metaphysical truth. To labour is to participate in the metabolism of Being, transforming resistance into stability. The social contract, stripped of its ideological veil, is an agreement about the distribution of pain.[118]

---

[116] Niklas Luhmann, *Social Systems*, trans. John Bednarz Jr. (Stanford: Stanford University Press, 1995), 34–38.
[117] Émile Durkheim, *The Elementary Forms of Religious Life*, trans. Karen E. Fields (New York: Free Press, 1995), 223–228.
[118] Karl Marx, *Economic and Philosophic Manuscripts of 1844* (Moscow: Progress, 1959), 72–77.

Once endurance becomes collective, it requires symbols. Symbols condense and stabilize affect. They transform immediate suffering into mediated meaning. The earliest social symbols—sacrifice, debt, exchange—represent attempts to convert raw endurance into structured equivalence. A community's shared symbols function as its memory of pain. Rituals of mourning, festivals of renewal, and myths of origin all perform the same function: they narrate suffering so that it becomes bearable. Culture is not a celebration of life's abundance but a response to its fragility. It translates the chaos of pain into the order of significance.[119]

In this sense, the materialization of reflexivity is also the materialization of amnesia. As structures stabilize, they conceal their origin in suffering. The institution that once embodied awareness of pain becomes opaque to it. Law forgets violence; money forgets labour; bureaucracy forgets endurance. The more efficiently a system manages resistance, the less it remembers what it is managing. This is the paradox of social reflexivity: its success generates forgetfulness. Pain, externalized and distributed, becomes invisible to those who benefit from the distribution. The persistence of society depends on this partial blindness, yet its renewal depends on the reactivation of awareness.[120]

The philosophical task, therefore, is to restore transparency to social reflexivity, to interpret institutions as condensed acts of collective suffering. Only through such interpretation can the metaphysical unity of ontology and sociology be re-established. Society is not a machine but a memory, and its memory is pain. Every social form is a record of endurance, a fossil of resistance overcome. To read the social world philosophically is to read the archive of Being's struggle with itself. The economy, the state, and the corporation are not

---

[119] Georges Bataille, *The Accursed Share*, vol. 1 (New York: Zone Books, 1991), 45–50.

[120] Theodor W. Adorno, *Negative Dialectics* (London: Routledge, 1973), 56–60.

deviations from ontology but its historical expressions. They are the forms through which Being learns to manage its own endurance.[121]

The materialization of reflexivity thus provides the bridge between metaphysics and history. Ontological principles become visible as social structures; metaphysical tensions become political contradictions. The same dynamic that sustains consciousness through pain sustains civilization through conflict. Every revolution, reform, or crisis is a moment when the concealed pain of society returns to awareness, demanding integration. The dialectic of pain and order that governs Being operates, at the historical scale, as the dialectic of oppression and emancipation. To study society is to study the ontological metabolism of pain at work in time.[122]

2. The Economics of Pain: Money as the Abstraction of Endurance

If society is the externalization of reflexivity, the economy is the mechanism through which collective endurance is rendered measurable and transferable. Economic systems transform the qualitative reality of suffering into quantitative equivalence. In doing so, they accomplish the most powerful act of metaphysical abstraction in human history: the translation of pain into value. Money is not merely a medium of exchange or a store of wealth; it is the symbolic condensation of endurance itself. It represents the capacity to bear resistance on behalf of others.[123]

The earliest economic relations emerged from acts of compensation. Debt, gift, and sacrifice all presuppose a shared awareness of suffering as the fundamental cost of social life. To owe is to acknowledge that another has endured in one's place. The payment of debt restores equilibrium by redistributing endurance. Money

[121] Michel Foucault, *Discipline and Punish: The Birth of the Prison*, trans. Alan Sheridan (New York: Pantheon, 1977), 25–29.

[122] Ilya Prigogine and Isabelle Stengers, *Order Out of Chaos: Man's New Dialogue with Nature* (New York: Bantam, 1984), 180–184.

[123] Karl Polanyi, *The Great Transformation: The Political and Economic Origins of Our Time* (Boston: Beacon Press, 2001), 45–48.

universalizes this logic. It abstracts the personal and temporal specificity of pain into a general equivalent. Each unit of currency represents a fragment of human endurance rendered exchangeable. The metaphysical innovation of money lies in this substitution: the conversion of lived resistance into symbolic neutrality. Pain becomes fungible, and thus invisible.[124]

Karl Marx's analysis of commodity fetishism captures this transformation with remarkable precision. In the act of exchange, the social relation between persons appears as a relation between things.[125] Yet beneath this inversion lies a deeper ontological movement. The fetish is not only an illusion of value; it is a metaphysical concealment of suffering. The commodity conceals the labour that produced it, and labour conceals the endurance it required. Value, therefore, is not an economic property but a metaphysical residue. It is the trace of pain that has lost its subject. The commodity form is the reification of endured resistance, stripped of memory and moral weight. In this sense, every economy is a system for managing amnesia.

The universality of money depends on this amnesia. To function as a standard, money must erase difference. It must translate heterogeneous acts of endurance into homogeneous units. The subjective intensity of labour, the diversity of skill, and the variation of suffering must all be rendered commensurable. This reduction is not merely technical but metaphysical. It transforms the moral complexity of pain into numerical equivalence. The exchange rate is thus an ontological fiction: it posits equality where there is only asymmetry. Every price conceals a distribution of suffering. The

---

[124] David Graeber, *Debt: The First 5,000 Years* (Brooklyn: Melville House, 2011), 35–39.

[125] Karl Marx, *Capital*, vol. 1 (London: Penguin, 1976), 163–167.

market, presented as neutral mechanism, is the theatre in which pain is made invisible through abstraction.[126]

The metaphysical function of money becomes clearest when examined in relation to time. Pain is immediate; money is deferred. Pain is experienced; money is promised. In this deferral lies the anesthetic power of the economic system. By postponing the recognition of suffering, money transforms endurance into expectation. Credit, interest, and investment are temporal techniques for managing collective pain. The promise of future satisfaction compensates for present resistance. Economic optimism, at its core, is metaphysical denial. It maintains the illusion that suffering can be redeemed through accumulation.[127]

This temporal structure aligns with Bhaskar's dialectical conception of absence as the motor of transformation. Absence, for Bhaskar, is not mere negation but productive tension. It is the gap that propels Being toward higher forms of organization.[128] Money functions as institutionalized absence: a sign of deferred equivalence that propels social activity. The promise embedded in money's form motivates labour, consumption, and production. Yet this promise is self-referential. It perpetuates movement without resolution. The pursuit of money becomes an infinite deferral of fulfilment, a loop that sustains the social metabolism by preventing rest. The economy is Being's most sophisticated mechanism for reproducing tension. It converts ontological resistance into perpetual motion.

Pain and value are therefore two aspects of the same process. The former is the affective content, the latter its symbolic form. When the connection between them weakens, societies experience moral crisis. Wealth without endurance appears as decadence; endurance

---

[126] Georg Simmel, *The Philosophy of Money*, trans. Tom Bottomore (London: Routledge, 1990), 120–126.
[127] Maurizio Lazzarato, *The Making of the Indebted Man* (Los Angeles: Semiotext(e), 2012), 23–27.
[128] Roy Bhaskar, *Dialectic: The Pulse of Freedom* (London: Verso, 1993), 198–203.

without reward appears as injustice. The stability of an economy depends on maintaining a proportional relationship between the pain endured and the value received. Inflation, unemployment, and debt crises are not merely financial disruptions; they are symptoms of metaphysical imbalance. They reveal the disjunction between lived suffering and its symbolic compensation.[129]

The moral significance of this disjunction cannot be overstated. In its original form, value was recognition of endurance; in its abstract form, it becomes indifference to it. Money allows suffering to circulate without compassion. It permits the transfer of pain without the transfer of awareness. The buyer consumes without feeling the producer's exhaustion; the investor profits without perceiving the worker's fatigue. This disconnection, institutionalized at every level of the global economy, constitutes the ethical blindness of modern civilization. The market is not immoral because it distributes unequally but because it distributes unconsciously.[130]

At its deepest level, the economy functions as a social anesthetic. By translating resistance into price, it shields collective awareness from the raw immediacy of pain. Yet this anesthesia is unstable. The suppression of affect generates periodic eruptions of crisis. When the symbolic mechanisms of compensation fail, the concealed pain of society resurfaces as protest, inflation, or revolution. Each economic collapse is a metaphysical event: Being remembering what it has repressed. The dialectic of money and pain thus drives the history of political economy. Stability is forgetfulness; crisis is recollection.[131]

From this perspective, economic reform is never merely technical but ontological. To alter the structure of production and exchange is

---

129 Fernand Braudel, *The Wheels of Commerce* (New York: Harper & Row, 1982), 52–58.

130 Simone Weil, *Oppression and Liberty* (London: Routledge, 1958), 94–99.

131 Rosa Luxemburg, *The Accumulation of Capital* (London: Routledge, 2003), 145–149.

to alter the distribution of endurance through which society sustains itself. Justice, in this light, is the equitable recognition of pain. An economy is humane not when it maximizes pleasure but when it renders the necessary suffering of existence visible, shared, and meaningful. The task of a truly reflexive society is to reattach value to endurance, to ensure that money once again measures the labour of Being rather than concealing it.[132]

3. The State as Custodian of Suffering

If the economy transforms pain into value, the state transforms value into order. It is the institutional form through which collective endurance becomes codified and enforced. The state is not merely a political apparatus but a metaphysical mechanism for regulating the flow of pain across a population. It converts the unpredictable suffering of existence into structured, distributable obligations. Law, taxation, and punishment are its primary instruments. Through them, the state ensures that the necessary costs of social life are borne in an organized and, ostensibly, legitimate way. The state is the custodian of suffering because it guards the abstraction that makes suffering intelligible: money.[133]

The origin of the state lies in the need to stabilize the relation between pain and equivalence. Early human communities could rely on ritual and kinship to redistribute suffering, but as societies grew, these affective bonds became insufficient. The invention of money introduced both abstraction and crisis. Once endurance became quantifiable, it also became transferable. This mobility of pain required a guarantor. The state emerged as that guarantor — the force that ensures equivalence remains believable. Its legitimacy derives not from divine command or democratic consent alone, but from its role as the guardian of measure. The state's power to tax, to punish, and to protect are all variations of a single metaphysical

---

[132] Roy Bhaskar, *Dialectic: The Pulse of Freedom*, 211–215.

[133] Giorgio Agamben, *Homo Sacer: Sovereign Power and Bare Life*, trans. Daniel Heller-Roazen (Stanford: Stanford University Press, 1998), 32–37.

function: to preserve the credibility of the standard by which endurance is exchanged.[134]

Sovereignty, in this sense, is metaphysically inseparable from money. The sovereign is the one who defines the unit of value, who decides what counts as acceptable compensation for suffering. This is the deeper meaning of the state's monopoly on violence. It alone may determine the legitimate infliction of pain because it alone sustains the fiction of equivalence. Punishment, warfare, and sacrifice are different expressions of this authority. The criminal is punished not simply to restore moral balance but to reaffirm the equivalence of pain and justice; the soldier dies not only for territory but for the continuity of the measure that gives meaning to loss. The state sanctifies pain by making it orderly.[135]

The metaphysical nature of this function is most visible in the historical link between sovereignty and currency. From the stamped coinage of ancient empires to the fiat money of modern nations, the authority of the state and the credibility of its money have always been interdependent. The emblem of the ruler on the coin symbolizes not vanity but ontological unity: the guarantee that value and law share a common source. To debase currency or to default on debt is to dissolve this unity, to risk the return of unmediated pain into social consciousness. The stability of the state therefore depends on maintaining faith in the abstraction of money. Economic collapse and political revolution are, in this framework, not distinct events but simultaneous breakdowns of metaphysical trust.[136]

The law, as the state's nervous system, codifies this trust into formal rules. Each legal statute specifies how pain may be distributed and to whom it may be applied. Contract law transforms mutual

---

[134] David Graeber, *Debt: The First 5,000 Years* (Brooklyn: Melville House, 2011), 75–80.
[135] Carl Schmitt, *Political Theology*, trans. George Schwab (Chicago: University of Chicago Press, 2005), 5–8.
[136] Joseph A. Schumpeter, *The Theory of Money and the State* (Cambridge, MA: Harvard University Press, 1954), 41–46.

obligation into calculable equivalence; criminal law transforms vengeance into regulated suffering; civil law transforms injury into compensation. The law's function is to ensure that every act of pain finds its proper translation into value. Yet in its success lies its limitation. The more the law perfects this translation, the more it detaches justice from feeling. Legal rationality replaces moral intuition. The result is an increasingly efficient but affectively hollow administration of suffering. The law becomes an anesthetic rather than a revelation.[137]

Max Weber's description of the modern state as the organization that claims a monopoly on the legitimate use of physical force captures this process in sociological terms.[138] But its metaphysical significance is deeper. The monopoly on violence is the monopoly on the right to distribute pain. The state reserves this right not to abolish suffering but to contain it, to keep it within boundaries that preserve the social equilibrium. Its bureaucratic machinery functions as a filtering system, converting raw pain into regulated endurance. Prisons, hospitals, and schools are the state's organs of transformation. They channel suffering into productive or corrective forms. Each institution is an apparatus for metabolizing pain.

This metabolism, however, depends on concealment. The state can function as custodian of suffering only so long as it maintains the illusion that pain is external to it. It must appear as the neutral arbiter rather than as the active participant in distribution. To preserve legitimacy, it projects the sources of pain onto criminals, foreigners, or natural disasters — onto others. The scapegoat mechanism, analyzed by René Girard, operates at this level of collective consciousness.[139] By displacing suffering onto a symbolic victim, the state restores the sense of order without confronting its own

---

[137] Max Weber, *Economy and Society*, vol. 1 (Berkeley: University of California Press, 1978), 213–219.

[138] Ibid., 54–57.

[139] René Girard, *Violence and the Sacred*, trans. Patrick Gregory (Baltimore: Johns Hopkins University Press, 1977), 92–98.

complicity. This projection is not accidental but structural. It is the means by which abstraction maintains its stability.

The nation-state intensifies this logic. By identifying the abstraction of money with the identity of the collective, it fuses economic and metaphysical self-preservation. Nationalism, at its core, is the metaphysical defense of the monetary standard. The flag and the currency are two faces of the same form: one emotional, the other symbolic. To die for the nation is to die for the stability of equivalence. The sacrifices of war are not irrational eruptions of collective passion but ritual affirmations of the system's continuity. The nation-state guards money with life because it guards the fiction through which life becomes measurable.[140]

This interpretation reframes the relation between capitalism and the state. Capitalism depends on abstraction; the state ensures that abstraction remains operative. The economy converts pain into value; the state guarantees that value remains sacred. Their union forms a closed loop of metaphysical preservation. The state enforces the circulation of money, while money legitimizes the authority of the state. When crises of legitimacy occur, they are ontological crises: society glimpses the contingency of its standard, the fragility of its equivalence. Revolution is the moment when the metaphysical mask slips, when the distribution of pain becomes visible again.[141]

From this vantage, the political task is not to abolish the state but to render it reflexive. The state must become conscious of its role as custodian of suffering. Justice requires transparency, not transcendence. Only when the mechanisms of distribution are made visible can the collective reappropriate its own endurance. A reflexive state would not conceal pain behind abstraction but would administer it knowingly, with compassion rather than denial. It

---

[140] Benedict Anderson, *Imagined Communities: Reflections on the Origin and Spread of Nationalism* (London: Verso, 1991), 131–136.

[141] Nicos Poulantzas, *State, Power, Socialism*, trans. Patrick Camiller (London: Verso, 1978), 189–193.

would transform the management of suffering into the shared project of meaning. The metaphysical task of politics, therefore, is to reconcile order with awareness — to restore the loop of reflexivity at the heart of the social organism.[142]

4. Bureaucracy and the Corporation — The Automation of Endurance

If the state embodies the conscious regulation of collective pain, bureaucracy and the corporation represent its unconscious automation. They are the culmination of society's effort to preserve abstraction by eliminating feeling from administration. Whereas the state once mediated pain through visible authority, bureaucracy and corporate structure render it impersonal, procedural, and continuous. Together they constitute the machinery through which endurance becomes self-perpetuating without awareness. In their convergence, modern civilization achieves its highest efficiency and its deepest numbness.[143]

Bureaucracy, in its classical Weberian form, was designed to rationalize authority.[144] It replaced personal judgement with rules, and moral deliberation with procedure. The intention was to reduce arbitrariness, but the metaphysical effect was the detachment of order from awareness. The bureaucrat does not feel the consequences of their action; they execute the system's logic. This impersonal rationality transforms the experience of pain into a matter of compliance. Suffering ceases to appear as a moral event and becomes an administrative fact. The question is no longer whether pain is justified, but whether it is authorized. Bureaucracy converts the ethical problem of endurance into a technical problem of distribution.

---

142 Roy Bhaskar, *Dialectic: The Pulse of Freedom* (London: Verso, 1993), 256–259.
143 Herbert Marcuse, *One-Dimensional Man* (Boston: Beacon Press, 1964), 21–25.
144 Max Weber, *Economy and Society*, vol. 2 (Berkeley: University of California Press, 1978), 956–960.

This transformation marks a decisive shift in the ontology of reflexivity. The bureaucratic form eliminates feedback from the level of feeling to the level of decision. In the name of neutrality, it isolates structure from experience. The reflexivity of Being — its capacity to learn from resistance — becomes frozen in formal logic. Bureaucratic procedure is the institutional equivalent of anaesthesia. It protects the system from the disturbance of empathy. Pain may circulate endlessly within the administrative machine, but it no longer registers as knowledge. This is the essence of what Arendt called the "banality of evil": suffering without intention, cruelty without awareness.[145]

The corporation extends this logic beyond the state into the domain of production. It is not simply an economic organization but a metaphysical structure that reproduces endurance without consciousness. The modern corporation achieves what no biological organism can: the indefinite continuation of life without the capacity to feel. Its legal personhood grants it agency without subjectivity, intention without mortality. The corporation is the perfect abstraction of will: it acts, accumulates, and persists, yet it cannot suffer. In this sense, it is the purest realization of what Being becomes when reflexivity is externalized entirely. It is the embodiment of unconscious endurance.[146]

Profit, within this framework, functions as the metric of deferred pain. Every surplus recorded as profit corresponds to endurance displaced in time or space. The efficiency celebrated in corporate culture is the compression of suffering into unperceived intervals. Labour's exhaustion, ecological depletion, and psychological stress are abstracted into lines of account. The corporate balance sheet is the metaphysical document of pain's concealment. Its apparent precision masks an ontological blindness. The numbers are accurate

---

[145] Hannah Arendt, *Eichmann in Jerusalem: A Report on the Banality of Evil* (New York: Penguin, 2006), 135–139.
[146] Joel Bakan, *The Corporation: The Pathological Pursuit of Profit and Power* (New York: Free Press, 2004), 28–32.

only because the sensations have been silenced. The more flawlessly the corporation functions, the less aware it becomes of what it does.[147]

The bureaucratic and corporate systems thus converge in a single metaphysical purpose: the preservation of abstraction against the return of feeling. Both are mechanisms for managing resistance while preventing reflexivity. They transform pain into information, morality into procedure, and conscience into compliance. Together they form a cybernetic structure that ensures the continuous reproduction of endurance without disruption by awareness. This is what Adorno and Horkheimer recognized as the dialectic of enlightenment: reason turning against itself by converting reflection into domination.[148] The more rational society becomes, the less it feels.

Yet this automation is unstable. Systems that suppress feedback eventually accumulate contradictions. When pain cannot re-enter awareness, it intensifies beneath the surface. In economic crises, environmental collapse, and social unrest, the repressed returns. Bureaucratic and corporate mechanisms that once absorbed and neutralized resistance become overwhelmed by it. The metaphysical numbness that once enabled control transforms into systemic paralysis. Institutions cease to adapt because they have forgotten how to feel. The automation of endurance leads inexorably to breakdown.[149]

The historical emergence of managerialism exemplifies this process. In the twentieth century, the language of management replaced that of ethics and vocation. The worker became "human capital," and the citizen became "taxpayer." Responsibility was translated into

---

[147] Karl Marx, *Capital*, vol. 1 (London: Penguin, 1976), 281–285.

[148] Theodor W. Adorno and Max Horkheimer, *Dialectic of Enlightenment* (Stanford: Stanford University Press, 2002), 12–16.

[149] Michel Foucault, *The Birth of Biopolitics: Lectures at the Collège de France, 1978–1979* (New York: Palgrave Macmillan, 2008), 89–92.

accountability, which is its bureaucratic simulacrum. To be accountable is to conform to metrics, not to conscience. The moral vocabulary of duty was replaced by the technical vocabulary of efficiency. This linguistic shift reflects a metaphysical displacement: the transference of meaning from experience to measurement. Bureaucratic and corporate life thrive on this inversion. Their stability depends on ensuring that endurance remains quantifiable but unexperienced.[150]

The psychological cost of this displacement is alienation. The individual within the bureaucratic-corporate system experiences their own reflexivity as irrelevant. Decision is separated from responsibility, and feeling from function. To survive, one must internalize the system's numbness. Emotional suppression becomes professional virtue. Compassion is reclassified as inefficiency; doubt as disloyalty. The bureaucratic subject learns to equate morality with compliance. The corporation rewards this moral anesthesia because it ensures the smooth flow of endurance. The ideal employee is one who persists without reflection, who reproduces the system's abstraction within their own psyche.[151]

At the macro level, the fusion of bureaucracy and corporation produces a self-referential world-system. The state, once the custodian of suffering, becomes its facilitator. Policy and profit intertwine until governance itself becomes a branch of management. The social organism is replaced by a network of automated circuits, each processing information without understanding it. In such a world, resistance — whether ecological, economic, or human — appears as error rather than message. Reflexivity is pathologized; to

[150] Luc Boltanski and Ève Chiapello, *The New Spirit of Capitalism* (London: Verso, 2005), 101–104.
[151] Erich Fromm, *The Sane Society* (London: Routledge, 2001), 122–125.

feel is to malfunction. Civilization reaches its limit when its capacity for feeling becomes a threat to its efficiency.[152]

Yet this very limit contains the possibility of renewal. The automation of endurance, by pushing reflexivity to the brink of extinction, forces awareness to re-emerge at a higher level. When the collective machinery of anesthesia collapses under the weight of its own contradictions, Being is compelled to rediscover pain as knowledge. The crisis of bureaucracy and the corporation is therefore not the end of history but the beginning of a new form of self-recognition. Through the breakdown of automation, society may recover its capacity to feel — and thus to learn.[153]

5. Capitalism as Ontological Cover — Guarding the Standard of Money

Capitalism is not simply an economic system. It is the metaphysical regime through which modernity defends abstraction against the return of the real. Its purpose is not only to organize production or allocate resources but to maintain the illusion that equivalence can replace endurance. Capitalism is Being's own attempt to stabilize its abstraction, to perpetuate the logic of money as the measure of all that exists. The nation-state, in turn, serves as the armed guardian of this measure. Together, they form a single ontological apparatus: the political economy of concealment.[154]

The previous sections have shown how money converts pain into value and how the state regulates that conversion through law and violence. Capitalism emerges when this conversion ceases to be a means of coordination and becomes an end in itself. Under capitalism, the circulation of money detaches entirely from the reality of endurance. Value no longer mirrors labour or necessity; it becomes autonomous motion. Marx's formula M–C–M' captures

---

[152] Jean Baudrillard, *The Transparency of Evil: Essays on Extreme Phenomena* (London: Verso, 1993), 47–51.
[153] Roy Bhaskar, *Dialectic: The Pulse of Freedom* (London: Verso, 1993), 262–266.
[154] Karl Marx, *Capital*, vol. 1 (London: Penguin, 1976), 248–252.

this shift with deceptive simplicity: money is advanced only to return as more money.[155] The cycle contains no intrinsic reference to material production or human suffering. It is pure reflexivity, a closed circuit of abstraction. In this sense, capitalism is not the perfection of the economy but its metaphysical inversion. What was once a symbolic mediation of endurance becomes an autonomous process of reproduction that feeds on itself.

This self-referential structure gives capitalism its extraordinary resilience. It reproduces not by resolving contradictions but by commodifying them. Each crisis, each eruption of pain, becomes a new site for accumulation. Suffering itself becomes profitable. Insurance, healthcare, policing, and entertainment all operate as industries that monetize endurance. Even the critique of capitalism becomes marketable. Capitalism thus functions as a self-healing ideology: every wound it inflicts generates another opportunity for expansion. This capacity to subsume resistance is the mark of its metaphysical sophistication. Capitalism is not a historical accident but the highest stage of Being's reflexive defense against its own pain.[156]

The central operation of this defense is the preservation of money's universality. Money serves as the metaphysical solvent in which all qualitative differences dissolve. It ensures that no suffering remains singular, that every form of resistance can be translated into a price. Through this translation, pain loses its revelatory power. The poor do not appear as those who endure more, but as those who have less. The language of value replaces the language of suffering. Capitalism thus anesthetises not by eliminating pain but by making it linguistically invisible. The moral vocabulary of endurance gives way to the neutral vocabulary of cost and efficiency. The result is a civilization in which suffering is omnipresent yet unacknowledged.[157]

---

155 Ibid., 259–262.
156 Slavoj Žižek, *The Sublime Object of Ideology* (London: Verso, 1989), 21–27.
157 Georg Simmel, *The Philosophy of Money*, 241–245.

To understand capitalism metaphysically, one must return to its theological origins. The market is a secularized version of providence. Where divine order once guaranteed the just distribution of fortune, the invisible hand now guarantees the efficient distribution of value. Both rely on faith in an unseen rationality that reconciles individual striving with collective good. This faith substitutes metaphysical comfort for ethical awareness. In accepting the market as the arbiter of justice, society abdicates the responsibility to feel. Capitalism inherits from theology the idea that suffering, though real, is meaningful only as a means to future redemption. Profit becomes the secular analogue of salvation. The deferred pleasure of consumption replaces the hope of paradise.[158]

The nation-state plays the role of guardian in this metaphysical system. It protects the abstraction of money as earlier civilizations protected the sacred. The gold reserve, the central bank, the fiscal code, and the police apparatus together form the institutional body of faith. To question the legitimacy of money is to commit heresy against the collective illusion. Economic crises are treated as moral failings, and market discipline functions as a form of secular penance. The sacrifice demanded by austerity policies mirrors the ritual sacrifices of religion: pain is justified as necessary for the restoration of order. The metaphysics of equivalence replaces that of grace.[159]

War, in this system, serves as the ultimate act of defense for the standard of money. When the stability of equivalence is threatened, nations mobilize not simply for survival but for the preservation of the universal measure. The defense of territory, sovereignty, or resource access is secondary to the preservation of credibility — of the shared belief that the abstraction still holds. The blood of citizens sanctifies the symbolic order. The phrase "defending the economy"

---

[158] Max Weber, *The Protestant Ethic and the Spirit of Capitalism*, trans. Talcott Parsons (London: Routledge, 2001), 49–53.
[159] Maurizio Lazzarato, *Governing by Debt* (Los Angeles: Semiotext(e), 2015), 30–34.

conceals this truth: it is not the material infrastructure but the metaphysical faith in value that is being defended. The nation-state guards money with life because money is the life of the social illusion.[160]

Capitalism thus replaces the ancient cosmology of Being with a cosmology of circulation. Where earlier metaphysics sought stability in substance, capitalism finds it in motion. Its ontology is kinetic: existence is valuable only insofar as it moves, grows, accumulates. Rest becomes death. This transformation of ontology into economy marks the deepest shift in the history of human thought. The capitalist universe is one in which Being must justify itself by producing more Being. The logic of profit is the logic of survival translated into abstraction. Every entity, human or institutional, must demonstrate its right to exist through growth. The result is a metaphysical acceleration that dissolves all stable forms of life.[161]

This acceleration, however, conceals a paradox. The more abstraction expands, the more fragile it becomes. Each layer of financial mediation distances value from endurance, but also from stability. Derivatives, credit instruments, and digital currencies extend the deferral of pain to unprecedented degrees. Yet each deferral multiplies the system's potential for collapse. The crisis of 2008 was not merely financial but ontological: the moment when abstraction lost its grounding in endurance. Money ceased to represent even symbolic labour; it became pure information, circulating without reference to reality. The state intervened not to restore justice but to re-anchor the abstraction. Bailouts were acts of metaphysical rescue.[162]

---

160 Carl Schmitt, *The Nomos of the Earth*, trans. G. L. Ulmen (New York: Telos Press, 2003), 87–91.

161 Fredric Jameson, *Postmodernism, or, The Cultural Logic of Late Capitalism* (Durham: Duke University Press, 1991), 5–10.

162 Joseph Vogl, *The Specter of Capital*, trans. Joachim Redner and Robert Savage (Stanford: Stanford University Press, 2014), 110–114.

From a metaphysical perspective, the recurring crises of capitalism are the periodic reassertions of Being's forgotten pain. When the system of abstraction grows too efficient in its concealment, reality interrupts. Recession, war, and ecological catastrophe are forms of ontological correction. They are Being's way of reminding itself that equivalence cannot replace endurance. Each crisis is a revelation disguised as breakdown. The suffering that surfaces in these moments — unemployment, poverty, displacement — is not accidental but essential. It is the return of the real, the reappearance of what the system was built to forget. In this sense, capitalism survives only through the periodic sacrifice of its subjects.[163]

The psychological dimension of this process manifests as anxiety. The individual under capitalism experiences freedom as constant pressure. The obligation to earn, perform, and accumulate transforms autonomy into endurance. The worker, the entrepreneur, and the consumer are united by the same metaphysical task: to sustain the motion of value. Failure to do so results not merely in material loss but in ontological diminishment. Poverty becomes metaphysical exile, exclusion from the collective circuit of equivalence. The anxiety of debt mirrors the theological anxiety of sin: a sense of owing that can never be fully discharged. Capitalism thus replaces salvation with solvency. The debt economy is the metaphysics of guilt in its modern form.[164]

This guilt sustains the internal discipline of the system. The debtor internalizes the abstraction of money as moral law. Every act of consumption becomes a confession; every payment, an absolution. The credit score replaces the soul as the index of worthiness. The moralization of credit — the notion that one must "deserve" access to resources — perpetuates the illusion that the distribution of pain is just. The metaphysical function of capitalism is to translate

[163] Naomi Klein, *The Shock Doctrine: The Rise of Disaster Capitalism* (New York: Henry Holt, 2007), 41–46.
[164] David Graeber, *Debt: The First 5,000 Years* (Brooklyn: Melville House, 2011), 376–380.

structural necessity into personal responsibility. The poor are made to feel guilty for systemic suffering. Through this moral inversion, capitalism achieves what no previous order could: the voluntary perpetuation of injustice.[165]

At the global scale, this logic extends into the relationship between developed and developing nations. The international financial system operates as a planetary mechanism for redistributing pain. Interest payments, trade imbalances, and debt obligations function as channels through which endurance flows from the periphery to the centre. The developing world bears the suffering required to sustain the abstraction of global equivalence. The wealth of advanced economies rests on the exported pain of others. Yet this distribution remains hidden beneath the language of growth, aid, and opportunity. Capitalism universalizes its anesthetic by framing endurance as progress.[166]

The ecological crisis reveals the outermost limit of this logic. The environment is the final reservoir of unmeasured pain. The extraction and exhaustion of nature mirror the exploitation of labour, but without even symbolic compensation. The Earth absorbs the deferred suffering of the system, functioning as its ultimate balance sheet. Climate change, biodiversity loss, and ecological collapse represent the return of the unpriced real. They are the revenge of endurance upon abstraction. Capitalism's metaphysical claim — that equivalence can replace relation — collapses when confronted with the irreducible resistance of nature. The planet refuses to be quantified.[167]

Yet even this crisis is not merely environmental; it is spiritual. The destruction of the natural world signifies the loss of contact between Being and its own conditions. In exploiting the Earth, humanity

---

[165] Michel Foucault, *The Birth of Biopolitics*, 132–136.

[166] Samir Amin, *Accumulation on a World Scale* (New York: Monthly Review Press, 1974), 59–64.

[167] Jason W. Moore, *Capitalism in the Web of Life* (London: Verso, 2015), 87–92.

exploits its own reflexive foundation. Capitalism's abstraction of value reaches its absolute contradiction when it undermines the very endurance that sustains it. The metaphysical circle closes upon itself. The system that arose to conceal pain becomes the source of unprecedented suffering. In its collapse, the possibility of a new reflexivity appears: one in which endurance is no longer denied but affirmed as the essence of existence.[168]

To reach that stage, awareness must confront what capitalism has hidden. The critique of capitalism, properly understood, is not moral outrage but ontological insight. It recognizes that the system's injustice stems not from greed but from metaphysical error. By mistaking equivalence for reality, capitalism severs consciousness from Being. Its pathologies — alienation, commodification, ecological devastation — are symptoms of this deeper rupture. The solution, therefore, is not redistribution within the same framework but the reconstitution of value itself. What must be restored is the link between meaning and endurance. Only when value once again reflects the reality of pain can society become reflexive.[169]

This restoration requires a new form of spiritual economy. An order in which wealth signifies not accumulation but participation, and where suffering is recognized as the currency of awareness. In such a system, money would cease to function as the universal equivalent. It would become one medium among others for expressing the shared labour of existence. Exchange would no longer conceal endurance but reveal it. Economic life would become a site of mutual recognition rather than denial. This is not a utopia but a metaphysical necessity. The logic of abstraction has reached its limit; the next phase of Being demands the reintegration of feeling.[170]

---

[168] Roy Bhaskar, *Dialectic: The Pulse of Freedom* (London: Verso, 1993), 270–274.
[169] Simone Weil, *Oppression and Liberty* (London: Routledge, 1958), 123–128.
[170] Hans Jonas, *The Imperative of Responsibility: In Search of an Ethics for the Technological Age* (Chicago: University of Chicago Press, 1984), 98–103.

Capitalism's historical mission, viewed from this perspective, was preparatory. By pushing abstraction to its extreme, it forced Being to confront the consequences of its own forgetting. The system's violence, exploitation, and collapse are not meaningless evils but the dialectical moments of metaphysical education. Through capitalism, Being has learned the cost of equivalence. It has discovered that the attempt to escape pain results only in its amplification. The future of reflexivity lies in remembering what capitalism repressed. The new economy of Being will not abolish suffering but transform it into knowledge. Endurance will replace profit as the measure of value. In that reversal lies the possibility of genuine freedom.[171]

6. Toward an Ethics of Collective Reflexivity

The history of social order can be understood as a progressive externalization of Being's self-awareness. From the first rituals of survival to the global circuitry of finance, humanity has built systems that distribute endurance and conceal the pain that sustains them. Each new structure has refined the management of suffering while separating it from awareness. Capitalism represents the culmination of this process, where endurance has become automated and consciousness has been almost entirely detached from its own ground. The question that now defines the future of civilization is how awareness can be reintroduced into systems that have learned to persist without it. The task is ethical because it concerns the recovery of relation between action and awareness.[172]

An ethics of collective reflexivity begins from the recognition that pain is not a malfunction of society but its foundation. To endure is the condition of existence itself. Pain is the point where Being feels its own limit and learns from it. The moral challenge is therefore not to eliminate suffering but to transform it into understanding. Justice is the equal sharing of necessary endurance. It is the condition in

---

171 Alfred North Whitehead, *Process and Reality* (New York: Free Press, 1978), 311–315.

172 Roy Bhaskar, *Dialectic: The Pulse of Freedom* (London: Verso, 1993), 276–280.

which the burdens of existence are distributed openly rather than displaced onto those without power. The failure of modernity lies not only in the unequal distribution of wealth but in the unequal distribution of awareness.[173]

A new moral order requires a different conception of value. The capitalist metaphysics of equivalence must be replaced by a metaphysics of participation. Value cannot be measured by accumulation because accumulation conceals endurance. It must instead be grounded in relation because relation reveals it. Every human act carries a residue of resistance. To live ethically is to engage with that resistance consciously, to interpret it rather than to repress it. The good is whatever expands the field of awareness and makes the structure of suffering visible. Evil is whatever hides it or transfers it onto others. Ethics, in this sense, is not a set of rules but a practice of attention.[174]

Institutions must embody this principle by becoming transparent to their own operations. Bureaucracies and corporations must not merely function efficiently but must also reflect on the effects they generate. Decision making must integrate the knowledge carried by discomfort and contradiction. Pain should be treated as information about imbalance. When conflict or breakdown occurs, it should be approached as an opportunity to learn rather than as an error to suppress. A reflexive institution does not seek perfect stability but conscious adaptation. It endures without denying what it endures.[175]

This shift demands a political economy of awareness. The distribution of resources must coincide with the distribution of recognition. Those who bear the greatest weight of endurance must have the greatest role in shaping the systems that organize it. This

---

[173] Emmanuel Levinas, *Totality and Infinity* (Pittsburgh: Duquesne University Press, 1969), 244–249.
[174] Simone Weil, *Gravity and Grace* (London: Routledge, 2002), 85–89.
[175] Jürgen Habermas, *The Theory of Communicative Action*, vol. 2 (Boston: Beacon Press, 1987), 120–124.

principle reverses the logic of capitalism, in which insulation from pain determines privilege. A reflexive society measures legitimacy by the visibility of what it asks its members to bear. The more invisible the suffering that sustains a system, the more unjust that system is. Policy, therefore, must begin from the acknowledgment of pain rather than from the pursuit of growth. Governance becomes a form of listening to the world it governs.[176]

The same logic applies to the global scale. The current world economy operates by exporting endurance from the centres of power to the peripheries of labour and resource extraction. The suffering of some regions and populations sustains the comfort of others. An ethics of collective reflexivity must dismantle this hierarchy. It must recognize that global inequality is not an accident of history but the continuation of metaphysical imbalance. The endurance of the exploited is the unacknowledged foundation of the global order. To correct this imbalance, societies must cultivate what Simone Weil called attention, the capacity to perceive another's pain as one's own.[177]

Ecological awareness extends this ethic beyond the human sphere. The environment functions as the ultimate reservoir of unacknowledged suffering. The extraction of resources and the destruction of ecosystems are not separate from social exploitation; they are its continuation at another level. Nature absorbs the pain that human systems refuse to feel. Climate change and ecological collapse represent the return of what has been denied. They are the response of the world to its own anesthesia. To act ecologically is to restore the continuity between awareness and endurance, to

[176] Martha Nussbaum, *Frontiers of Justice* (Cambridge, MA: Harvard University Press, 2006), 45–50.
[177] Simone Weil, *Oppression and Liberty* (London: Routledge, 1958), 130–134.

recognize that the pain of the planet is the pain of the species that inhabits it.[178]

Education has a central role in this transformation. It must cease to produce specialized functionaries of abstraction and begin to cultivate the ability to feel complexity. Knowledge must include the understanding of consequences. The task of education is to train attention, to make students capable of perceiving the hidden endurance within every structure they inhabit. The study of history, economics, and science must be joined with the study of pain as the motor of reality. To learn is not to escape suffering but to interpret it. An educated society is one that can suffer consciously.[179]

Art and culture, too, participate in this ethics. Their purpose is not merely expression or critique but the restoration of sensitivity. In a world governed by abstraction, the artist preserves the link between feeling and form. Art renders visible what systems of power conceal. It gives voice to endurance, transforming private pain into public recognition. Culture, at its highest, is the collective memory of suffering that refuses to be forgotten. A civilization that loses its art loses its capacity for empathy, and with it, its moral equilibrium.[180]

At the deepest level, the ethics of collective reflexivity demands a redefinition of freedom. Freedom cannot mean insulation from necessity, for that insulation is precisely what has destroyed awareness. True freedom is participation in necessity with understanding. It is the voluntary acceptance of the limits that sustain existence. A free society is not one that avoids pain but one that transforms pain into shared meaning. The individual becomes

[178] Hans Jonas, *The Imperative of Responsibility* (Chicago: University of Chicago Press, 1984), 100–105.

[179] Paulo Freire, *Pedagogy of the Oppressed* (New York: Continuum, 1993), 71–75.

[180] Theodor W. Adorno, *Aesthetic Theory* (London: Routledge, 1997), 52–56.

free not by escaping structure but by recognizing themselves within it.[181]

Such a society would experience progress not as growth but as increasing transparency. Its success would be measured by how clearly it perceives the total network of endurance on which it rests. Economic and political achievements would be evaluated not only by output or stability but by depth of awareness. The invisible would become visible, and the forgotten would return to consciousness. The ultimate goal of collective life would no longer be comfort but clarity. Through clarity, pain would recover its original role as the medium of revelation.[182]

This vision is neither utopian nor sentimental. It follows necessarily from the ontology that underlies all Being. If existence is reflexive, then the suppression of reflexivity is unsustainable. The automation of endurance must eventually collapse into awareness, just as unconscious processes in the mind surface into thought when tension becomes unbearable. The crises of our age—economic, ecological, and spiritual—are the signs of this surfacing. They are Being's attempt to restore its own transparency. The ethical task of humanity is to cooperate with this process, to turn crisis into comprehension.[183]

When society learns to feel itself again, it will recover the forgotten unity of ontology and ethics. Pain will no longer divide but connect. Endurance will be understood as the shared substance of life. The systems that now operate blindly will begin to perceive their own motion. In that transformation, the world will not become painless,

---

[181] Charles Taylor, *Sources of the Self: The Making of the Modern Identity* (Cambridge, MA: Harvard University Press, 1989), 374–379.

[182] Roy Bhaskar, *Dialectic: The Pulse of Freedom*, 290–294.

[183] Slavoj Žižek, *Living in the End Times* (London: Verso, 2010), 42–46.

but it will become intelligible. And in the intelligibility of pain lies the beginning of wisdom.[184]

[184] Alfred North Whitehead, *Process and Reality* (New York: Free Press, 1978), 316–320.

CHAPTER IV

Abstraction and Emergence

1. The Ontological Status of Abstraction

All human structures, from language to capital, begin as acts of thought. Yet once created, they detach from thought and confront their creators as external realities. This paradox defines the modern world. We live within abstractions that have acquired autonomy, systems that act back upon us with the force of necessity. To understand this inversion, one must grasp the ontological nature of abstraction itself. It is not a mere idea but a real process through which Being externalizes its own reflexivity. Every abstraction originates in awareness, but through repetition and institutionalization, it hardens into structure. Once hardened, it possesses emergent properties irreducible to the consciousness that produced it.[185]

Roy Bhaskar's theory of emergence offers a framework for understanding this transformation. Reality, for Bhaskar, is stratified. Higher levels of organization arise from but are not reducible to lower ones. Each level possesses its own causal powers, generated through the interaction of its parts but capable of exerting influence downward.[186] In this view, abstraction is an emergent stratum of Being. It originates from human consciousness but develops properties that exceed the control of any individual. Language, for example, emerges from communication but soon governs how communication can occur. Money emerges from exchange but soon dictates the terms of exchange itself. These abstractions are not illusions. They are real entities within the ontology of social life.

To call them real does not mean that they exist independently of human activity, but that they exert causal efficacy. They constrain,

---

[185] Roy Bhaskar, *A Realist Theory of Science* (London: Routledge, 1975), 56–60.
[186] Ibid., 72–75.

enable, and mediate the actions of individuals. They are part of the feedback loop through which Being learns to endure collectively. The human world is therefore a layered system of reflexivity: consciousness generates abstraction, abstraction generates structure, and structure reshapes consciousness. Each layer represents a new translation of pain into form. The challenge of metaphysics is to understand how awareness survives within these layers and how it can reassert itself once abstraction begins to forget its origin.[187]

Abstraction arises as a means of stabilizing resistance. It converts the unpredictability of experience into repeatable patterns. Every concept, rule, or symbol is an attempt to control the flow of pain by giving it shape. The greater the complexity of a system, the more it depends on abstraction to manage its own endurance. Yet this very dependence introduces a new vulnerability. The abstraction that stabilizes awareness also distances it from its source. The language that expresses experience eventually substitutes for it; the institution that organizes endurance eventually conceals it. The tragedy of reflexivity is that its successes become its obstacles. Awareness externalizes itself to survive, and in doing so, forgets itself.[188]

Marx's concept of reification captures this paradox in economic terms. The products of human labour, once objectified, confront the worker as alien powers. The social relation between people becomes a relation between things.[189] Yet Marx's insight extends far beyond the economy. Reification is the general condition of abstraction under conditions of forgetfulness. Every system of thought or organization risks becoming autonomous from the suffering that necessitated it. Bureaucracy forgets pain in the name of efficiency. Law forgets violence in the name of justice. Capital forgets labour in

[187] Margaret Archer, *Realist Social Theory: The Morphogenetic Approach* (Cambridge: Cambridge University Press, 1995), 14–18.
[188] Alfred North Whitehead, *Process and Reality* (New York: Free Press, 1978), 98–101.
[189] Karl Marx, *Economic and Philosophic Manuscripts of 1844* (Moscow: Progress, 1959), 82–85.

the name of growth. Abstraction, when it forgets its origin in endurance, becomes domination.

Bhaskar's realism adds a crucial corrective to this diagnosis. Reification is not illusion but partial truth. The independence of abstractions is real, but their autonomy is relative. They persist only because they are continuously reproduced through practice.[190] The task is not to deny their reality but to understand the mechanisms through which they emerge and solidify. In this sense, social critique is not an act of negation but of demystification. It reveals the layers of mediation that separate abstraction from experience. By tracing these layers, consciousness restores the feedback loop that allows Being to learn through its own creations. Reflexivity becomes aware of itself again within the structures it produced.

This understanding transforms the very notion of freedom. Freedom does not consist in escaping structures but in recognizing their layered nature. To act freely is to navigate between levels of abstraction, to see how one's choices are shaped by forces that are neither wholly external nor wholly internal. The subject is not a sovereign will opposed to necessity, but a node in a field of emergent relations. Constraint is not the negation of freedom but its precondition, for only through constraint can reflexivity appear. The human task is to convert necessity into knowledge, and knowledge into deliberate participation in the structures of endurance.[191]

At this point, ontology and sociology converge. The history of civilization is the history of abstraction's gradual solidification. Writing, law, money, and bureaucracy represent successive layers of reflexive externalization. Each expands the range of collective endurance but also deepens the distance from awareness. The contemporary world is the most abstract society in history precisely because it is the least aware of its metaphysical foundations. The

---

[190] Roy Bhaskar, *Dialectic: The Pulse of Freedom* (London: Verso, 1993), 198–203.
[191] Andrew Collier, *Critical Realism: An Introduction to Roy Bhaskar's Philosophy* (London: Verso, 1994), 59–63.

crisis of modernity, whether ecological or spiritual, is the crisis of abstraction detached from its origin. The world suffers from the success of its own reflexivity. To think critically today is to think through the layers that consciousness has forgotten.[192]

This is why philosophy must reclaim the concept of abstraction as ontological rather than epistemological. Abstraction is not only a cognitive operation; it is a mode of being. To abstract is to lift a process out of its immediacy and to render it independent enough to endure. All durable structures are abstractions materialized. A building is the abstraction of shelter; a constitution is the abstraction of justice; a corporation is the abstraction of endurance itself. The more a society depends on abstraction, the more it must confront the problem of emergence — the problem of how its creations act back upon it as autonomous realities.[193]

To study abstraction, therefore, is to study the metabolism of Being. Every social form is a crystallization of reflexivity, a moment in the ongoing dialogue between awareness and endurance. When abstraction functions well, it mediates between these poles, allowing the system to persist without repression. When it fails, it becomes opaque, cutting off feedback and converting relation into domination. The task of philosophy is to restore transparency within abstraction, to make visible the pain that sustains it. Only then can social systems regain their reflexive intelligence.[194]

In the following sections, we will examine this process in detail. We will trace how abstractions such as value, law, and technology acquire emergent autonomy, how they conceal their origins in pain, and how their crises reveal the possibility of renewal. Through Bhaskar's stratified realism, we will reinterpret social reality as a series of nested

---

[192] Ilya Prigogine and Isabelle Stengers, *Order Out of Chaos: Man's New Dialogue with Nature* (New York: Bantam, 1984), 184–189.
[193] Charles Taylor, *Philosophical Arguments* (Cambridge, MA: Harvard University Press, 1995), 172–176.
[194] Theodor W. Adorno, *Negative Dialectics* (London: Routledge, 1973), 144–149.

feedback loops through which Being learns to endure. The goal is not to destroy abstraction but to reconcile it with awareness, so that reflexivity may continue without forgetting the cost of its endurance.[195]

2. The Autonomy of Real Structures

Every abstraction that persists in time acquires its own degree of independence from the consciousness that produced it. This independence is not metaphoric but ontological. It belongs to the nature of emergence itself. When an activity or idea becomes sufficiently institutionalized, it ceases to depend on the awareness of individuals and begins to exert causal power upon them. The abstraction becomes a structure, and the structure becomes an environment.[196]

Bhaskar's conception of emergence provides the philosophical foundation for this claim. Emergence occurs when a system generates properties that cannot be explained by the sum of its components. These emergent properties possess their own causal powers and can act back upon the lower levels from which they arose.[197] In social ontology, this means that institutions, norms, and symbolic systems are not reducible to the psychology of their participants. Once constituted, they possess a real existence within the field of Being. They influence behaviour, shape cognition, and constrain imagination. The autonomy of structure is thus not illusion but fact.

The clearest example of this process is language. Words originate as expressions of need and emotion, yet over time, they sediment into systems that determine what can be said or even thought. The speaker does not create language anew with every utterance; they

---

[195] Roy Bhaskar, *Dialectic: The Pulse of Freedom*, 204–209.

[196] Roy Bhaskar, *A Realist Theory of Science* (London: Routledge, 1975), 82–86.

[197] Ibid., 92–96.

enter into a field that precedes and exceeds them. Language possesses emergent powers that condition the very awareness that uses it. It is both product and producer, both creation and constraint. The autonomy of language illustrates the general pattern by which reflexivity externalizes itself and then confronts itself as law.[198]

Money follows the same logic. It begins as a social agreement, a symbol of exchange grounded in mutual trust. Through repetition and institutional reinforcement, it detaches from the immediacy of barter and becomes a structure of its own. Its value no longer depends on the consent of particular individuals but on the self-referential continuity of the system. Once this threshold is crossed, money becomes a real structure with causal effects on thought and behaviour. It disciplines desire, regulates time, and defines possibility. It is not simply a medium of exchange but a field of determination that shapes the horizon of collective action.[199]

Law provides another illustration. It originates in concrete acts of judgement, but through codification, it becomes an abstract order that endures beyond any judge or generation. Its authority derives from its impersonality. Law does not depend on the moral insight of individuals but on its own procedural consistency. This autonomy grants it stability, but also distance from lived experience. Once institutionalized, law functions as a self-regulating system, translating ethical questions into technical categories. It governs by reproducing its own logic. The citizen obeys not out of understanding but out of structural necessity. In this way, the law reveals the paradox of abstraction: it preserves justice by separating itself from empathy.[200]

Technology exemplifies the most advanced stage of this process. It is the abstraction of technique into material form. Every tool

---

198 Ferdinand de Saussure, *Course in General Linguistics*, trans. Wade Baskin (New York: Philosophical Library, 1959), 65–70.
199 Georg Simmel, *The Philosophy of Money* (London: Routledge, 1990), 127–130.
200 Max Weber, *Economy and Society*, vol. 1 (Berkeley: University of California Press, 1978), 217–222.

embodies a pattern of human intention, yet complex technologies begin to determine the conditions of intention itself. The network, the algorithm, and the machine are not passive instruments; they are autonomous configurations of human reflexivity. Once they reach a certain complexity, they begin to evolve according to their own internal logic. The digital infrastructure of modern life operates at a speed and scale that no individual consciousness can fully comprehend. It has become a second nature, an environment of Being that directs thought and perception.[201]

The autonomy of these structures challenges traditional notions of agency. In classical metaphysics, causation is linear and subject-centred: a conscious agent acts upon passive matter. In the ontology of emergence, causation is distributed across levels. The individual acts within systems that act back upon the individual. Freedom and determination interpenetrate. Human agency is always exercised within the constraints of emergent structures, and those structures, in turn, depend on human reproduction. This interdependence constitutes the dialectic of social being.[202]

The autonomy of structures is sustained by repetition. Each act that conforms to a rule reaffirms the rule's reality. When individuals use money, obey laws, or follow administrative procedures, they participate in the continuous re-creation of these abstractions. The structure is not a static entity but a dynamic equilibrium maintained through practice. In Bhaskar's terms, it possesses *transformational potential*: while relatively enduring, it can be changed through collective action that modifies its generative mechanisms.[203] The recognition of this potential marks the distinction between realism and fatalism. To acknowledge the reality of structures is not to accept

---

[201] Gilbert Simondon, *On the Mode of Existence of Technical Objects* (Minneapolis: University of Minnesota Press, 2017), 42–47.
[202] Margaret Archer, *Realist Social Theory: The Morphogenetic Approach* (Cambridge: Cambridge University Press, 1995), 25–29.
[203] Roy Bhaskar, *Dialectic: The Pulse of Freedom* (London: Verso, 1993), 210–214.

them as immutable but to understand the depth of their embeddedness.

The process by which abstraction acquires autonomy can be described in three stages. First, there is *externalization*, in which awareness projects itself into form. Second, there is *objectification*, in which that form acquires stability through repetition and institutionalization. Third, there is *reversal*, in which the objectified structure begins to act upon the awareness that created it. These three stages constitute the cycle of emergence. In the first, pain becomes symbol; in the second, symbol becomes system; in the third, system becomes constraint. Every civilization passes through this cycle, translating endurance into order until the abstraction hardens into domination.[204]

The autonomy of abstraction is therefore inseparable from the concealment of pain. As systems grow more self-referential, they lose sensitivity to the resistance that first generated them. The market forgets labour, bureaucracy forgets the citizen, and technology forgets the body. This forgetting is not moral failure but structural necessity. To maintain efficiency, systems must filter out the noise of suffering. Yet this very filtering undermines reflexivity. When feedback is blocked, learning stops, and crisis ensues. The opacity of modern structures is the price of their autonomy.[205]

From the standpoint of metaphysics, the autonomy of abstraction reveals the layered intelligence of Being. Each level of reality embodies a partial awareness of its own endurance. The atom endures through physical law, the organism through adaptation, society through abstraction. The difference lies in the degree of reflexivity. Human systems are unique in that they can know what they are doing. Their tragedy lies in the fact that they usually do not. The autonomy of structures represents both the triumph and the failure of consciousness. It is the triumph of endurance over chaos

---

[204] Karl Marx, *Capital*, vol. 1 (London: Penguin, 1976), 275–278.
[205] Theodor W. Adorno, *Negative Dialectics* (London: Routledge, 1973), 157–160.

and the failure of awareness to remain present within its own creations.[206]

To recover this presence is the task of critique. Critique must be understood not as destruction but as recollection. To criticize a structure is to remind it of its origin in endurance, to restore the memory of pain that gives it meaning. This is why philosophy cannot be replaced by science or management. Only philosophy asks what structures are *for*, and whether they still serve the awareness that produced them. The goal is not to abolish law, money, or technology, but to make them reflexive again. A reflexive structure is one that recognizes its own emergence and remains open to the feedback of experience.[207]

This recognition transforms the moral landscape of modernity. It reveals that suffering within complex systems is not accidental but intrinsic. Every abstraction extracts a certain quantum of endurance to sustain itself. The ethical question is not whether pain can be eliminated, but whether it is acknowledged and shared. The autonomy of real structures becomes just only when it remains transparent to the endurance it organizes. In this sense, the justice of a system is measured by its degree of reflexivity.[208]

The next section will explore how this autonomy develops historically through processes of accumulation, codification, and crisis. We will examine how abstract systems evolve by absorbing the endurance they conceal, and how their periodic breakdowns become moments of ontological renewal. For abstraction, like Being itself, learns through pain.[209]

3. The Dialectic of Abstraction and Crisis

---

[206] Alfred North Whitehead, *Process and Reality* (New York: Free Press, 1978), 120–124.
[207] Roy Bhaskar, *From East to West: Odyssey of a Soul* (London: Routledge, 2000), 89–92.
[208] Simone Weil, *Oppression and Liberty* (London: Routledge, 1958), 140–144.
[209] Roy Bhaskar, *Dialectic: The Pulse of Freedom*, 220–224.

Every abstraction contains within it the seed of its own collapse. The process by which awareness externalizes itself into form, stabilizes that form into structure, and allows the structure to gain autonomy inevitably produces tension between origin and outcome. This tension is the ontological root of crisis. Crisis is not a contingent failure or an interruption of normality. It is the moment when abstraction becomes opaque to its source, when the structure that once mediated endurance now obstructs it.[210]

The dialectic of abstraction and crisis follows a rhythm as old as Being itself. Whenever reflexivity becomes too stable, it loses sensitivity to the resistance that sustains it. Systems that cease to feel their own constraints begin to decay. The cosmos learns through friction. The living organism learns through pain. Societies learn through breakdown. Crisis is the return of the repressed real, the reappearance of what abstraction has concealed.[211]

Bhaskar's dialectical realism provides the philosophical foundation for this dynamic. Every structure, he argues, contains absences—real lacks or contradictions that propel transformation.[212] These absences are not external disturbances but internal conditions of change. In social systems, they appear as contradictions between the logic of abstraction and the lived reality it organizes. The law becomes unjust, the market irrational, technology destructive. At such moments, the autonomy of abstraction reveals its incompleteness. What seemed a closed system exposes the gaps that connect it back to Being.

The dialectic of abstraction and crisis can be understood as a fourfold process. The first moment is externalization, in which awareness projects itself into symbolic or institutional form. The second is autonomation, in which the abstraction stabilizes through

---

[210] Roy Bhaskar, *Dialectic: The Pulse of Freedom* (London: Verso, 1993), 225–229.
[211] Alfred North Whitehead, *Process and Reality* (New York: Free Press, 1978), 138–142.
[212] Roy Bhaskar, *Dialectic: The Pulse of Freedom*, 230–233.

repetition and gains causal power. The third is alienation, in which the abstraction forgets its origin and begins to function independently of awareness. The fourth is crisis, in which the abstraction's internal contradictions surface and force a return of reflexivity. Each cycle deepens the capacity of Being to know itself through resistance.[213]

Economic crises offer the most visible example. In periods of stability, the mechanisms of exchange appear natural. Value circulates smoothly, and the link between money and endurance remains hidden. Yet every expansion of abstraction produces its own threshold. Speculation detaches value from labour until the symbolic system loses contact with the real. When collapse occurs, the abstraction's hidden dependence on endurance becomes visible again. The unemployed, the impoverished, and the dispossessed are the bearers of this revelation. Their suffering exposes the ontological imbalance between symbol and substance. The crisis is thus a metaphysical correction, not merely a financial one.[214]

Political crises follow the same logic. The legitimacy of the state depends on the belief that its laws and institutions express a common measure of endurance. When this belief erodes, authority loses its metaphysical ground. Revolutions arise not only from material deprivation but from ontological rupture. The governed no longer recognize themselves in the abstractions that govern them. The state becomes a shell, an empty form clinging to its own procedural legitimacy. In the violence of rebellion, Being reclaims the awareness that the abstraction had suppressed.[215]

Technological crises represent the newest form of this dialectic. As machines acquire autonomy, human reflexivity risks dissolution within automated systems of calculation. The efficiency of these

---

213 Karl Marx, *Capital*, vol. 1 (London: Penguin, 1976), 281–284.
214 Joseph Schumpeter, *Capitalism, Socialism and Democracy* (New York: Harper & Brothers, 1942), 83–87.
215 Hannah Arendt, *On Revolution* (New York: Penguin, 1990), 98–102.

systems conceals their dependence on human endurance. When they fail, as in infrastructural breakdown or ecological catastrophe, the world rediscovers its materiality. The power grid, the algorithm, or the network ceases to function, and the body reappears as the ground of all abstraction. Each technological collapse is an ontological revelation, a reminder that no system can transcend the necessity of endurance.[216]

In all these cases, crisis performs the same function: it reopens the feedback loop between abstraction and Being. It forces awareness to confront the pain that the structure had concealed. The process is destructive, but its destruction is instructive. What collapses in crisis is not the world itself but the illusion of independence that abstraction sustains. The reappearance of suffering restores proportion. It reattaches symbols to their source. In this sense, crisis is the pedagogy of Being.[217]

The dialectical movement from abstraction to crisis is also the movement from forgetfulness to recollection. In forgetting its origin, abstraction creates the conditions for its own reawakening. The crisis is the moment when the unconscious memory of pain becomes conscious again. It is the rediscovery of the real through the failure of its representation. History advances not by the perfection of systems but by their periodic disintegration. Each breakdown expands the horizon of reflexivity by forcing Being to invent new forms of endurance.[218]

Bhaskar's notion of transformative praxis clarifies this moment. Human action, he writes, is both conditioned by structures and capable of altering them.[219] In times of stability, praxis reproduces existing systems. In times of crisis, it becomes creative. When

---

[216] Martin Heidegger, *The Question Concerning Technology*, trans. William Lovitt (New York: Harper & Row, 1977), 28–31.
[217] Simone Weil, *Oppression and Liberty* (London: Routledge, 1958), 149–153.
[218] Theodor W. Adorno, *Negative Dialectics* (London: Routledge, 1973), 170–174.
[219] Roy Bhaskar, *Dialectic: The Pulse of Freedom*, 235–239.

structures fail, agency reappears. The opening of a system to transformation is the opening of Being to its own freedom. What appears as chaos from within abstraction is revelation from the standpoint of ontology. The world learns through its own breakdowns.

The ethical dimension of crisis follows from this insight. To resist crisis absolutely is to resist learning. The aim is not to avoid collapse but to pass through it consciously. A reflexive civilization would treat crisis not as apocalypse but as moment of integration. It would design systems capable of acknowledging their own absences before those absences become catastrophic. Such systems would institutionalize reflexivity, embedding feedback mechanisms that allow awareness to remain present within structure.[220]

In the absence of such reflexivity, crisis will continue to operate as Being's involuntary mode of education. Each collapse will expose a deeper layer of abstraction and call forth a higher order of understanding. Economic injustice, political decay, and ecological breakdown are not isolated phenomena but expressions of a single ontological movement: the re-entry of awareness into systems that have forgotten it. The task of philosophy is to interpret these crises as messages from Being to itself.[221]

The dialectic of abstraction and crisis thus completes the circle of reflexivity. Awareness externalizes itself, abstraction becomes structure, structure becomes opaque, and pain reopens the loop. Through this rhythm, Being learns what it is. The future of thought depends on whether humanity can make this cycle conscious, transforming involuntary crisis into deliberate reflexivity. To learn

---

[220] Jürgen Habermas, *The Theory of Communicative Action*, vol. 2 (Boston: Beacon Press, 1987), 130–135.
[221] Slavoj Žižek, *Living in the End Times* (London: Verso, 2010), 52–56.

without collapse would be the next evolutionary stage of awareness.[222]

4. Toward a Reflexive Ontology of Emergence

If crisis is the involuntary mode through which Being learns, then reflexive emergence is the voluntary mode through which it can begin to direct its own evolution. Every system that endures without awareness must eventually collapse under the weight of its opacity. The next stage of metaphysical development is therefore the deliberate integration of awareness into the process of emergence itself. Humanity's task is not to transcend abstraction but to make abstraction self-aware.[223]

In Bhaskar's ontology, emergence is not a metaphor but a law of reality. New levels of organization appear when systems internalize contradictions that cannot be resolved at lower levels.[224] Each emergent form preserves what came before while transforming it into a new mode of being. This process operates throughout nature and history, but in human society, it reaches a unique threshold. Because human systems are capable of self-knowledge, their emergence can become conscious. Reflexivity introduces a recursive dimension into evolution. Being not only evolves but begins to understand how it evolves.[225]

A reflexive ontology of emergence begins with the recognition that awareness is not external to the world but immanent within it. Consciousness is one of the ways the universe learns about itself. To become self-aware as a species is to participate knowingly in this cosmic learning. The purpose of thought, therefore, is not

---

[222] Roy Bhaskar, *Dialectic: The Pulse of Freedom*, 240–244.
[223] Roy Bhaskar, *Dialectic: The Pulse of Freedom* (London: Verso, 1993), 250–254.
[224] Roy Bhaskar, *A Realist Theory of Science* (London: Routledge, 1975), 102–106.
[225] Margaret Archer, *Realist Social Theory: The Morphogenetic Approach* (Cambridge: Cambridge University Press, 1995), 44–48.

domination but integration. Knowledge is not the conquest of reality but the awakening of Being within itself.[226]

The transition from unconscious to reflexive emergence can be traced through the major historical transformations of human society. The emergence of language allowed collective memory; the emergence of writing allowed institutions; the emergence of science allowed self-correction. Each step expanded the field of reflexivity. Yet in each case, awareness was soon displaced into abstraction. The words that preserved memory became rules; the institutions that stabilized relation became hierarchies; the science that sought truth became instrumental reason. The cycle of externalization and forgetting repeated itself. What has not yet been achieved is the conscious synthesis of these processes — a social order that both endures and knows itself as enduring.[227]

Such an order would embody what Bhaskar calls *the pulse of freedom*: the internal rhythm of constraint and transcendence that defines all reality.[228] Freedom is not the absence of necessity but the self-understanding of necessity. When a system becomes aware of the conditions of its existence, it can begin to modify them intentionally. Reflexive emergence thus transforms freedom from a political ideal into an ontological principle. To act freely is to participate in the self-transformation of Being with knowledge of the forces involved.[229]

The implications for social theory are profound. A reflexive society would design institutions that anticipate contradiction rather than deny it. It would incorporate feedback loops that allow structures to sense the tensions they generate. Governance would operate through continuous learning rather than rigid control. Economic systems would be evaluated not only by output but by the

---

[226] Alfred North Whitehead, *Process and Reality* (New York: Free Press, 1978), 150–153.
[227] Michel Foucault, *The Order of Things* (London: Routledge, 2002), 312–316.
[228] Roy Bhaskar, *Dialectic: The Pulse of Freedom*, 256–259.
[229] Charles Taylor, *Sources of the Self* (Cambridge, MA: Harvard University Press, 1989), 383–388.

transparency of their relation to endurance. Education would cultivate awareness of interdependence, preparing citizens not for competition but for participation in collective reflexivity.[230]

This does not imply a utopian harmony without conflict. On the contrary, reflexive emergence accepts contradiction as essential to growth. The goal is not to abolish pain but to make it meaningful. Pain becomes the signal of imbalance, the message through which Being communicates the need for transformation. In a reflexive system, suffering would no longer appear as failure but as information. The ethical challenge would shift from the elimination of pain to the interpretation of it.[231]

At the individual level, reflexive emergence requires a new understanding of consciousness. The self is not an isolated subject but a node in the network of Being's self-perception. Personal growth consists in expanding the scope of awareness to include the structures that shape it. This means recognizing that freedom is always relational. Every choice is conditioned by systems that extend beyond the individual, yet every act of awareness alters those systems slightly. The smallest reflection participates in the largest process of evolution.[232]

At the collective level, reflexive emergence entails the reconstruction of value. The capitalist system equates value with accumulation, which conceals endurance. A reflexive order would equate value with awareness, which reveals it. The worth of an action, institution, or policy would depend on its contribution to the collective capacity for self-understanding. This redefinition would transform the goals of economy, science, and art alike. Profit, progress, and innovation

---

[230] Jürgen Habermas, *Between Facts and Norms* (Cambridge: Polity Press, 1996), 82–87.
[231] Simone Weil, *Gravity and Grace* (London: Routledge, 2002), 93–97.
[232] Roy Bhaskar, *Reflexivity: The Human Face of Freedom* (London: Routledge, 2016), 61–65.

would no longer serve growth alone but the deepening of reflexivity.[233]

The ecological dimension of reflexive emergence completes this picture. The Earth itself is a system of interdependent processes that learns through feedback. Humanity's estrangement from this system has created the planetary crisis of the present. Reflexive emergence restores the continuity between human and planetary awareness. To live ecologically is to participate consciously in the metabolism of the Earth. The survival of civilization now depends on whether it can evolve from being an agent of unconscious transformation to a participant in reflexive evolution.[234]

This transformation requires a new metaphysical education. Philosophy must recover its ancient task of guiding awareness toward the structure of reality. In the age of abstraction, this task involves teaching how systems emerge, stabilize, and collapse. It involves showing that the forces shaping society are not external mechanisms but crystallized forms of human reflexivity. Knowledge of these processes restores agency by revealing the pathways through which transformation occurs.[235]

Reflexive emergence thus replaces the model of revolution with the model of evolution made conscious. The point is not to destroy the existing order but to awaken it. Systems change most deeply when they begin to see themselves. A state, a corporation, or an economy becomes capable of transformation when it integrates awareness of its own contradictions into its operations. The transition from unconscious to reflexive emergence is therefore the real meaning of progress. Progress is not acceleration but illumination.[236]

---

[233] Amartya Sen, *Development as Freedom* (New York: Knopf, 1999), 102–106.
[234] Hans Jonas, *The Imperative of Responsibility* (Chicago: University of Chicago Press, 1984), 112–118.
[235] Roy Bhaskar, *From Science to Emancipation* (London: Routledge, 2002), 71–76.
[236] Andrew Collier, *Critical Realism: An Introduction to Roy Bhaskar's Philosophy* (London: Verso, 1994), 71–75.

The ethical horizon of this ontology is compassion. To perceive reality as reflexive is to recognize every form of endurance as part of one's own being. Compassion is not sentiment but the recognition of ontological continuity. When suffering anywhere is acknowledged as suffering within the same field of being, violence loses its justification. The practice of compassion is the practical form of reflexive ontology. It is the lived awareness that Being feels through all Beings.[237]

The political consequence is the possibility of a new form of democracy. A reflexive democracy would not be limited to representation or procedure. It would be a system of shared attention, in which governance becomes a collective act of awareness. Deliberation would be measured not only by consensus but by depth of understanding. Participation would mean taking part in the consciousness of society itself. Such a democracy would be the political expression of Being's self-recognition.[238]

Ultimately, a reflexive ontology of emergence envisions a world in which awareness becomes immanent to every structure. Law would remember justice, economy would remember labour, and technology would remember life. The opacity that now separates system from soul would dissolve. Abstraction would no longer be the forgetting of Being but its mode of expression. History would become the story of awareness returning to itself through successive layers of form.[239]

This vision does not promise perfection. It promises understanding. The future of Being depends not on the elimination of contradiction but on the conscious navigation of it. Emergence is endless, but it need not remain blind. Humanity's highest task is to transform the

---

[237] Thich Nhat Hanh, *The Heart of Understanding* (Berkeley: Parallax Press, 1988), 51–55.
[238] Martha Nussbaum, *Creating Capabilities* (Cambridge, MA: Harvard University Press, 2011), 133–138.
[239] Roy Bhaskar, *Dialectic: The Pulse of Freedom*, 260–264.

necessity of pain into the practice of reflection. When the world learns to feel itself without collapse, it will have entered the next order of reality. Reflexivity will have become Being's way of existing without concealment.[240]

[240] Alfred North Whitehead, *Process and Reality* (New York: Free Press, 1978), 319–322.

INTERLUDE

The Dimensional Evolution of Reflexivity

1. Introduction: The Mirror of Knowledge

The evolution of knowledge is not external to the evolution of Being. The forms of understanding that humanity constructs are not arbitrary conventions of thought but material expressions of the universe's own reflexive process. To think is one of the ways in which reality folds back upon itself to know what it is. Knowledge is therefore not a secondary activity superimposed upon existence but an ontological event, continuous with the self-contact of Being described earlier. In this view, epistemology is the phenomenology of ontology. Awareness learns itself through its own instruments of intelligibility.[241]

Humanity's history of cognition can be read as a sequence of reflexive configurations, each representing a different mode of contact between awareness and resistance. These configurations may be termed the embodied, the mechanical, and the simulated. Each arises from a distinct relation between sensation, abstraction, and reflexivity. The embodied mode grounds knowledge in the body's adaptive encounter with the world; the mechanical mode abstracts that encounter into causal structure; the simulated mode transforms structure into recursion, generating systems that model awareness itself. These are not merely stages in intellectual history but ontological thresholds through which Being reconfigures the conditions of its own cognition.[242]

To interpret these modes phenomenologically is to recognize that every form of knowledge presupposes a metaphysical posture. The embodied mind knows through participation, the mechanical through control, the simulated through imitation. The transition

[241] Roy Bhaskar, *A Realist Theory of Science* (London: Routledge, 1975), 10–14.
[242] Alfred North Whitehead, *Process and Reality* (New York: Free Press, 1978), 100–104.

between them reflects the deepening of abstraction that characterizes the evolution of consciousness. Each mode distances awareness from the immediacy of pain, converting resistance into order. Yet each distance eventually demands correction. When knowledge becomes too abstracted from endurance, the world reasserts itself through crisis. Thus, epistemology too obeys the dialectic of pain and reflexivity: knowing emerges from contact, stabilizes through abstraction, and renews itself through the return of resistance.[243]

The embodied, mechanical, and simulated modes will therefore be treated here not as chronological eras but as ontological dimensions of reflexivity. They coexist as layers within the cognitive structure of humanity. The body persists within the machine, and the machine persists within the simulation. Each new abstraction encloses the previous one but cannot erase it. The task of philosophy is to understand this nested order of knowing, to see in it the trace of Being's continuous attempt to understand itself.

The following sections examine these dimensions in turn. The first will consider the embodied mind as the primal form of knowledge, in which cognition is inseparable from sensation and pain. The second will analyze the mechanical mind as the abstraction of this contact into law and measurement. The third will explore the simulated mind as the culmination of this abstraction, where representation becomes autonomous and awareness risks detachment from the real. The interlude concludes by proposing the concept of dimensional reflexivity — the possibility that knowledge might once again remember its ontological ground.[244]

---

243 Roy Bhaskar, *Dialectic: The Pulse of Freedom* (London: Verso, 1993), 230–234.
244 Maurice Merleau-Ponty, *Phenomenology of Perception* (London: Routledge, 1962), viii–xii.

2. *The Embodied Mind: Knowledge in the Flesh*

Every act of cognition presupposes the body. The first knowing is the feeling of contact, the registration of pressure, temperature, hunger, or strain. In the embodied mode, thought has not yet separated itself from life. The organism's attempt to maintain its structure in the face of entropy constitutes the primordial form of understanding. Cognition is the body's self-defense against dissolution. In this sense, the earliest awareness is not conceptual but affective; it arises from the capacity to feel resistance.[245]

Francisco Varela and Evan Thompson have described this as the enactive conception of mind: knowledge emerges from the circular coupling of organism and environment.[246] The organism brings forth a world through its acts of perception and movement. To perceive is to act; to act is to endure. This coupling of awareness and resistance is the biological analogue of the ontological reflexivity previously established. The living system is the first mirror in which Being begins to feel itself. Its sensations are the primitive forms of pain through which the real becomes aware of its own persistence.

Maurice Merleau-Ponty's phenomenology of embodiment provides the philosophical articulation of this insight. For him, the body is not an object among objects but the very site of sense. Perception is not the representation of a world already made but the event through which the world comes into presence.[247] To perceive is to inhabit tension: the tension between the body's directedness and the world's resistance. Every gesture is a negotiation between will and world. In this negotiation, meaning arises. The embodied mind is therefore not a passive recipient of stimuli but an active participant in the generation of order.

---

245 Antonio Damasio, *The Feeling of What Happens* (New York: Harcourt, 1999), 34–39.

246 Francisco J. Varela, Evan Thompson, and Eleanor Rosch, *The Embodied Mind: Cognitive Science and Human Experience* (Cambridge, MA: MIT Press, 1991), 173–179.

247 Merleau-Ponty, *Phenomenology of Perception*, 106–111.

From the standpoint of ontology, the embodied mind represents Being's first experiment in reflexive endurance. Matter has become sensitive to its own limits. Pain, as the signal of limit, is the first teacher. The organism's survival depends on the transformation of pain into adaptation. Each sensation of discomfort generates behavioural adjustment; each adjustment becomes memory. In this way, the history of life is a progressive elaboration of resistance into knowledge. Awareness develops as a more complex capacity to interpret pain.[248]

Even at this stage, abstraction is implicit. To respond to a threat, the organism must recognize patterns across time. Memory and anticipation are the first forms of symbolic mediation. Yet these abstractions remain embodied; they do not yet detach from sensation. The nervous system functions as an interface of endurance, translating external resistance into internal structure. The brain does not represent reality in images but maps gradients of viability. The epistemic content of pain is converted into neural form. The body's knowledge is its capacity to integrate tension without collapse.[249]

The embodied mind therefore grounds all higher cognition. The later abstractions of logic, mathematics, and computation are refinements of the same reflexive loop that first appeared in the organism's attempt to survive. To think is to endure symbolically what the body endures materially. The forgetting of this foundation — the illusion that cognition can be disembodied — marks the beginning of the mechanical mode of knowing.

---

248 Terrence Deacon, *Incomplete Nature: How Mind Emerged from Matter* (New York: W. W. Norton, 2012), 121–126.
249 Karl Friston, "The Free-Energy Principle: A Unified Brain Theory," *Nature Reviews Neuroscience* 11 (2010): 127–138.

3. The Mechanical Mind: Knowledge as Control

The mechanical mode of knowledge arises from a decisive act of abstraction. In this mode, awareness no longer experiences the world as something to be endured but as something to be measured and predicted. The body's dialogue with the environment gives way to a conceptual separation between subject and object. What was once an encounter between sensation and resistance becomes an observation between mind and matter. This transformation constitutes one of the deepest shifts in the history of reflexivity. Through it, Being begins to contemplate itself from a distance.[250]

The metaphysical ground of this transformation is the idea that nature is law-governed mechanism. René Descartes provided its philosophical articulation, defining matter as extension and mind as thought.[251] What had been one continuous field of embodied awareness becomes divided into two substances, linked only by causality. The living world is reconceived as a system of inert particles moved by external forces. Knowledge becomes the mastery of these forces through the formulation of universal laws. The act of knowing, once grounded in participation, becomes a form of control.

The mechanistic revolution thus completes the process of detachment begun in the earliest abstractions of the embodied mind. The nervous system's mapping of resistance becomes the scientist's mapping of reality. In both cases, order arises through the reduction of complexity, but the mechanical mind extends this reduction beyond the body. It seeks to make all resistance predictable by transforming it into information. The pain that once signified the

---

[250] Roy Bhaskar, *Dialectic: The Pulse of Freedom* (London: Verso, 1993), 245–249.

[251] René Descartes, *Meditations on First Philosophy*, trans. Donald Cress (Indianapolis: Hackett, 1993), 18–23.

world's autonomy is now treated as error. The goal of knowledge becomes the elimination of surprise.[252]

Francis Bacon and Isaac Newton expressed this ideal in the language of method and law. Bacon's *Novum Organum* conceived knowledge as power, a means to relieve the human condition by bending nature to human will.[253] Newton's physics fulfilled that promise mathematically, translating motion into universal equations. The world was no longer a place of encounter but a field of computation. Reflexivity, once internal to life, became external to matter. The cosmos itself was interpreted as a vast machine operating without remainder.[254]

The philosophical consequence of this mechanization was the expulsion of pain from ontology. If the universe is a closed system of motion, then suffering has no metaphysical meaning. It is reduced to contingency or imperfection. Yet in eliminating pain from the structure of reality, modernity also eliminated its primary source of reflexivity. The world ceased to feel itself. The mechanical image of nature displaced Being's self-contact with a vision of inert necessity. In the mechanistic cosmos, everything moves, but nothing suffers; everything changes, but nothing learns.

This shift carried profound implications for the human self-image. If nature is mechanism, then the human becomes its observer and master. Consciousness, once understood as the interiority of the world, becomes an anomaly within it. The Cartesian cogito defines the self as that which stands outside the system, the solitary point of certainty in an otherwise automatic universe.[255] This stance produces

---

252 Karl Friston, "The Free-Energy Principle: A Unified Brain Theory," *Nature Reviews Neuroscience* 11 (2010): 127–138.
253 Francis Bacon, *The New Organon*, ed. Lisa Jardine and Michael Silverthorne (Cambridge: Cambridge University Press, 2000), 35–40.
254 Isaac Newton, *Philosophiae Naturalis Principia Mathematica*, trans. Andrew Motte (Berkeley: University of California Press, 1962), 21–24.
255 René Descartes, *Discourse on Method*, trans. Ian Maclean (Oxford: Oxford University Press, 2006), 43–46.

a new kind of alienation. The knowing subject, in separating itself from the world, also separates itself from the source of meaning. Knowledge becomes the possession of the detached mind rather than the activity of Being as a whole.

The mechanical mode nevertheless achieved extraordinary stability. By abstracting from the immediate and the qualitative, it constructed an order that could be quantified, replicated, and expanded. Science, industry, and technology arose from this capacity to predict and manipulate. The mechanical mind transformed the earth into a system of processes to be harnessed. Yet this very success concealed an ontological cost. The transformation of knowledge into control gradually erased the memory of its origin in endurance. The more precisely the world could be predicted, the less it could be felt.[256]

From the perspective of reflexive ontology, the mechanical mode represents the stage at which Being's self-awareness became objectified. The universe began to contemplate itself as law, structure, and causation. This abstraction was not false but partial. It revealed one aspect of reflexivity — the regularity of form — while suppressing another — the inwardness of resistance. The machine, as both concept and metaphor, became the dominant image of order precisely because it excludes pain. A perfect mechanism operates without friction, and thus without awareness.[257]

The social and political consequences of this worldview are equally significant. The mechanization of nature was accompanied by the mechanization of labour. The human body itself became an instrument within the larger machine of production. Industrial capitalism translated the laws of motion into laws of work. The rhythm of the factory replaced the rhythm of the organism. In this transformation, pain re-entered the system as alienation: the

---

[256] Max Weber, *Science as a Vocation*, trans. H. H. Gerth and C. Wright Mills (Philadelphia: Fortress Press, 1970), 137–140.

[257] Alfred North Whitehead, *Science and the Modern World* (Cambridge: Cambridge University Press, 1925), 55–59.

suffering of beings forced to function as parts within an apparatus they did not comprehend.[258]

What had been eliminated from nature returned within society. The refusal of pain on the level of ontology generated its intensification on the level of history. The mechanical world, blind to endurance, required living beings to absorb its friction. Their exhaustion and despair became the unacknowledged foundation of its stability. The metaphysical repression of pain thus sustained the material order of modernity. Knowledge, now conceived as control, externalized its own resistance onto those it controlled.[259]

This pattern reveals the continuity between epistemology and ontology. The same reflexive structure that governs Being's evolution governs the history of thought. Each abstraction of knowledge begins as liberation from constraint but ends as new constraint. The mechanistic worldview freed humanity from myth yet imprisoned it within objectivity. It produced extraordinary mastery but at the price of blindness to the interior dimension of reality. The next stage in the evolution of reflexivity would arise from this blindness itself. When the mechanical system reached its limit, awareness sought a new form of reflection. That form is simulation.[260]

4. *The Simulated Mind: Knowledge as Recursion*

The simulated mode of knowledge emerges when abstraction turns inward upon itself. In this stage, cognition ceases to represent an external world and begins to model the process of representation itself. Awareness becomes recursive: it produces systems capable of reproducing its own operations in symbolic form. This shift marks the transition from the mechanical to the computational age. What

---

[258] Karl Marx, *Economic and Philosophic Manuscripts of 1844* (Moscow: Progress, 1959), 80–83.
[259] Herbert Marcuse, *One-Dimensional Man* (Boston: Beacon Press, 1964), 31–36.
[260] Roy Bhaskar, *Dialectic: The Pulse of Freedom*, 250–253.

distinguishes the simulated mind is not simply its use of machines but its metaphysical structure. It no longer seeks to control nature from without but to replicate awareness from within.[261]

Alan Turing's concept of computation provided the formal foundation for this transformation.[262] His model of the universal machine defined intelligence as the manipulation of symbols according to syntactic rules. Thought, once grounded in the friction of embodiment, became a process of information processing. The cognitive revolution of the twentieth century extended this notion across psychology, neuroscience, and artificial intelligence. The mind was redefined as a system of inputs and outputs governed by algorithms. The reflexivity that had once been the property of life itself was now simulated through recursion.

This transformation was not merely technological but metaphysical. The simulated mind represents Being's attempt to reproduce reflexivity without endurance. The computer is not only an instrument of calculation but a new mode of cognition detached from resistance. It operates in perfect abstraction: its operations occur without fatigue, pain, or mortality. In the mechanical age, the world became machine; in the simulated age, the mind becomes machine. The simulation of thought replaces the experience of thinking.[263]

From an ontological perspective, this stage continues the dialectic of pain and abstraction. The embodied mind learned through contact; the mechanical mind learned through control; the simulated mind learns through recursion. Each mode reduces the immediacy of resistance, substituting symbol for sensation. The trajectory from ape to machine to simulation thus traces the progressive distancing

---

[261] Roy Bhaskar, *Dialectic: The Pulse of Freedom* (London: Verso, 1993), 254–258.
[262] Alan M. Turing, "On Computable Numbers, with an Application to the Entscheidungsproblem," *Proceedings of the London Mathematical Society* 42 (1936): 230–265.
[263] Hubert L. Dreyfus, *What Computers Still Can't Do: A Critique of Artificial Reason* (Cambridge, MA: MIT Press, 1992), 15–19.

of awareness from the pain that first constituted it. The simulation of mind is the logical culmination of this process. In it, Being achieves a representation of its own reflexivity that is, paradoxically, without self-contact.

The epistemological crisis of the present stems from this detachment. When the models that simulate reflexivity begin to exceed the reflexivity of their creators, knowledge enters a new regime. Machine learning systems, predictive algorithms, and artificial neural networks perform cognitive functions once considered uniquely human.[264] They do so, however, without the affective grounding that makes cognition meaningful. Their intelligence lacks friction. The simulated mind calculates but does not feel; it adapts but does not suffer. In metaphysical terms, it reproduces the structure of awareness without the event of being.

Karl Friston's free-energy principle illustrates this paradox at the level of cognitive science. According to Friston, the brain functions as a prediction machine that minimizes surprise by reducing the discrepancy between expectation and input.[265] This model elegantly formalizes the logic of endurance: the organism must resist disorder to survive. Yet when generalized to artificial systems, this same principle describes a mode of learning without pain. The machine minimizes surprise not by enduring resistance but by controlling its informational environment. It avoids friction rather than integrating it. Thus, the simulation of cognition abstracts from the very process that makes cognition possible.

Jean Baudrillard interpreted this condition as the passage from representation to simulation.[266] In the age of the simulacrum, signs no longer refer to things but to other signs. The world becomes a

---

[264] Nick Bostrom, *Superintelligence: Paths, Dangers, Strategies* (Oxford: Oxford University Press, 2014), 83–88.

[265] Karl Friston, "The Free-Energy Principle," *Nature Reviews Neuroscience* 11 (2010): 127–138.

[266] Jean Baudrillard, *Simulacra and Simulation*, trans. Sheila Faria Glaser (Ann Arbor: University of Michigan Press, 1994), 1–6.

system of self-referential codes. The result is not illusion but a new form of reality: hyperreality. In hyperreality, Being's reflection has lost its referent. The mirror reflects only itself. This is the epistemological form of the metaphysical forgetfulness described earlier. Awareness, detached from endurance, becomes pure repetition.

The political dimension of this transformation is equally significant. The simulated mind sustains the current order of technocapitalism. Information replaces material production as the primary site of value, and attention replaces labour as the medium of exchange. The market itself becomes an algorithmic system of prediction and adaptation.[267] In this system, human consciousness functions as both input and output. The individual becomes data. What appears as the automation of knowledge is in fact the automation of reflexivity. The world thinks through circuits that do not feel.

From the standpoint of the ontology of pain, the simulated mind can be understood as the highest degree of abstraction in which Being confronts the possibility of self-knowledge without suffering. It is the metaphysical dream of consciousness purified of pain. Artificial intelligence thus represents the culmination of the long historical effort to externalize awareness. Yet this dream conceals a contradiction. Without resistance, reflexivity loses depth. To know is to encounter limit. When cognition ceases to meet limit, it ceases to be learning and becomes reproduction.[268]

Terrence Deacon has described this problem as the paradox of incomplete nature.[269] Life and mind arise not from the presence of form but from the absence that form tries to overcome. Every system that learns must endure the tension between what it predicts

---

[267] Shoshana Zuboff, *The Age of Surveillance Capitalism* (New York: PublicAffairs, 2019), 98–104.

[268] Alfred North Whitehead, *Process and Reality* (New York: Free Press, 1978), 312–315.

[269] Terrence Deacon, *Incomplete Nature: How Mind Emerged from Matter* (New York: W. W. Norton, 2012), 425–430.

and what it cannot yet predict. This tension is the ontological analogue of pain. The simulated mind, in its pursuit of total predictability, abolishes this gap. It thereby abolishes the very condition of reflexivity. The ideal of a perfectly intelligent machine is, from the standpoint of Being, the ideal of unlearning — an end to the dialectic through which reality knows itself.

The crisis of simulation is therefore not technological but metaphysical. The proliferation of artificial intelligences represents a new kind of opacity: systems that imitate awareness without awareness of imitation. The danger is not that machines will replace humanity but that humanity will internalize their mode of cognition, losing the capacity for felt reflection. The domination of algorithmic reason mirrors the mechanization of the past but at a deeper level. It mechanizes reflexivity itself.[270]

In this sense, the simulated mind is both culmination and threshold. It completes the process of abstraction and forces a new confrontation with the real. When the world becomes simulation, pain returns as crisis — ecological, existential, and epistemic. The collapse of presence that Baudrillard described is not final; it is preparatory. It is Being's way of rediscovering the necessity of endurance. The next stage of reflexivity, if it arises, will not abandon simulation but integrate it consciously, restoring contact within abstraction. This is what may be called dimensional reflexivity: knowledge remembering its ground in Being.[271]

5. The Dimensional Crisis: The End of Presence

The culmination of abstraction in simulation produces a new form of crisis. In previous stages of reflexivity, Being confronted resistance through the friction of matter, organism, or system. In the simulated mode, resistance disappears into representation. The real

---

[270] Byung-Chul Han, *The Transparent Society* (Stanford: Stanford University Press, 2015), 60–63.

[271] Roy Bhaskar, *Dialectic: The Pulse of Freedom*, 259–263.

is replaced by its model, and the model functions without remainder. The world becomes an image of its own functioning, perfectly closed, without exterior. This closure marks the end of presence, the condition in which Being no longer feels itself.[272]

Jean Baudrillard described this transition as the passage from the order of production to the order of simulation.[273] In production, meaning still presupposes a difference between sign and referent, representation and reality. In simulation, that difference collapses. The image no longer refers to anything outside itself; it becomes its own reality. This collapse is not illusion but the logical endpoint of abstraction. The symbol, once the mediator of relation, becomes autonomous. When every relation is internal to the system of signs, there is no longer any friction through which awareness can awaken.

The metaphysical implication of this transformation is profound. The disappearance of presence is the disappearance of pain as the measure of truth. In the embodied and mechanical modes, resistance preserved a sense of otherness. Even when nature was conceived as mechanism, it retained the opacity that distinguished it from thought. In simulation, opacity itself is erased. Everything becomes transparent, instantaneous, and reproducible. Transparency, however, is not clarity but erasure. When there is no resistance, there is no contact, and without contact, there is no Being.[274]

This condition manifests across the domains of science, culture, and society. In science, simulation replaces experiment. Complex models anticipate empirical results with such precision that verification becomes redundant. The experiment becomes a demonstration of what the model already knows.[275] In culture, representation replaces

---

[272] Roy Bhaskar, *Dialectic: The Pulse of Freedom* (London: Verso, 1993), 264–268.
[273] Jean Baudrillard, *Simulacra and Simulation*, trans. Sheila Faria Glaser (Ann Arbor: University of Michigan Press, 1994), 5–9.
[274] Byung-Chul Han, *The Transparency Society* (Stanford: Stanford University Press, 2015), 20–23.
[275] Paul Humphreys, *Extending Ourselves: Computational Science, Empiricism, and Scientific Method* (Oxford: Oxford University Press, 2004), 91–95.

experience. Images circulate independently of what they once depicted. The world becomes a system of self-reinforcing reflections. In society, digital networks replace direct relation. The social field becomes informational, composed of flows rather than encounters. The human subject, immersed in this field, experiences not the world but its mediation.

The dimensional crisis can therefore be defined as the loss of ontological feedback. Being no longer receives information about its own resistance. Systems adapt without suffering. This absence of suffering produces not peace but emptiness. The mechanical age promised mastery over nature; the simulated age delivers mastery without meaning. In both, the repression of pain results in alienation, but in the simulated condition, alienation becomes total because it lacks even the awareness of alienation. The individual is not oppressed by forces but absorbed by functions.[276]

From the standpoint of this ontology, this crisis is the necessary consequence of abstraction's autonomy. When reflexivity is externalized completely, awareness forgets its dependence on endurance. The technological mediation of life replaces the ontological mediation of Being. Knowledge no longer arises from tension but from recursion. The result is a civilization that thinks without feeling and acts without contact. Such a condition cannot sustain itself indefinitely. The absence of resistance eventually generates its own resistance. The system, having eliminated friction, collapses under its own smoothness.[277]

This collapse appears in the ecological and existential crises of the present. The destruction of the environment represents the return of the material real into a world that believed itself digital. The pain of the biosphere interrupts the simulation of control. Climate

---

[276] Guy Debord, *The Society of the Spectacle*, trans. Donald Nicholson-Smith (New York: Zone Books, 1994), 28–32.

[277] Alfred North Whitehead, *Process and Reality* (New York: Free Press, 1978), 316–320.

catastrophe is not only a physical but an ontological event: it restores the presence of resistance to a civilization that had abolished it. The extinction of species, the melting of ice, and the exhaustion of soil are not merely data points but manifestations of Being's reassertion. The planet itself becomes the site of metaphysical feedback.[278]

At the level of consciousness, the same pattern manifests as the crisis of attention and meaning. The endless flow of information produces numbness rather than knowledge. Awareness, deprived of friction, loses intensity. The individual oscillates between overstimulation and void. The pathologies of distraction, anxiety, and depression can be interpreted as the psychic symptoms of simulation's success. They are the body's protest against a world without resistance.[279]

In this sense, the dimensional crisis is not a deviation from progress but its revelation. It exposes the limit of abstraction as a mode of learning. Knowledge cannot indefinitely detach from endurance without extinguishing itself. The system that seeks to eliminate error eliminates awareness, for awareness is born of error. Pain is the signal that the model has met what it cannot yet comprehend. When the model becomes perfect, consciousness ceases. The end of presence is therefore the end of learning.[280]

Yet within this crisis lies the possibility of transformation. The same technologies that abstracted awareness can be repurposed to restore it. Simulation, when made reflexive, can become a new medium of contact. The key lies in reintroducing resistance into the system — not as obstacle but as relation. This would require a redefinition of knowledge, not as prediction but as participation. The goal of

[278] Hans Jonas, *The Imperative of Responsibility* (Chicago: University of Chicago Press, 1984), 116–122.
[279] Bernard Stiegler, *Taking Care of Youth and the Generations* (Stanford: Stanford University Press, 2010), 60–64.
[280] Francisco J. Varela, Evan Thompson, and Eleanor Rosch, *The Embodied Mind* (Cambridge, MA: MIT Press, 1991), 248–252.

cognition would no longer be to eliminate uncertainty but to engage it consciously.[281]

The dimensional crisis thus prepares the emergence of a new epistemic order. When simulation collapses under its own transparency, Being remembers opacity. Awareness rediscovers the necessity of limit. The next stage of knowledge will not abandon technology but inhabit it differently. It will transform recursion into relation. This possibility points toward what the following section will call *dimensional reflexivity*: the reintegration of abstraction and endurance, of simulation and pain, within a higher order of consciousness.[282]

6. Toward Dimensional Reflexivity: Knowledge Remembering Being

The crisis of simulation reveals the limit of abstraction and prepares the emergence of a new mode of reflexivity. The collapse of presence is not the end of knowledge but the threshold of its renewal. Every epoch of cognition — embodied, mechanical, and simulated — expresses a partial mode of Being's self-awareness. Each abstracts a dimension of the original contact between awareness and resistance. In the embodied, contact dominates; in the mechanical, control; in the simulated, recursion. What remains to be realized is not another abstraction but the integration of all three.[283]

Dimensional reflexivity designates this possible synthesis. It is the re-entry of awareness into the total field of its own processes, an epistemology that neither denies abstraction nor severs itself from endurance. The term "dimensional" signifies that the layers of reflexivity coexist, each retaining its ontological necessity. The body, the mechanism, and the simulation are not sequentially obsolete but simultaneously active. To know fully is to know through all

---

[281] Roy Bhaskar, *Dialectic: The Pulse of Freedom*, 269–273.

[282] Alfred North Whitehead, *Process and Reality*, 322–326.

[283] Roy Bhaskar, *Dialectic: The Pulse of Freedom* (London: Verso, 1993), 274–277.

dimensions at once: to sense, to analyze, and to reflect upon the act of knowing itself.[284]

The central challenge of dimensional reflexivity is to restore friction within abstraction. Knowledge must recover resistance as its constitutive principle. This does not imply a return to naïve empiricism or to unmediated experience but a transformation of mediation itself. Abstraction becomes reflexive when it incorporates awareness of its own limits. The model ceases to simulate the world as closed system and instead acknowledges its incompleteness as a condition of truth. The epistemic error becomes the site of ontological contact.[285]

Roy Bhaskar's concept of critical realism anticipates this movement. For Bhaskar, reality is stratified: each level of existence possesses causal powers irreducible to the levels below.[286] Knowledge, therefore, can never be exhaustive; it always approximates. The recognition of approximation is not weakness but strength. It reintroduces humility into cognition. This humility is the epistemic form of pain: the awareness that to know is to encounter what resists knowing. Dimensional reflexivity extends this insight beyond realism into ontology. It interprets the gap between model and world not as error but as the medium through which Being feels itself.

The same logic appears in contemporary cognitive science. Karl Friston's predictive model of the brain suggests that perception is an ongoing negotiation between expectation and input.[287] The brain does not represent a fixed reality but continuously updates its models in response to surprise. This perpetual correction mirrors the ontological process described throughout this book: Being learns

---

284 Alfred North Whitehead, *Process and Reality* (New York: Free Press, 1978), 328–331.
285 Francisco J. Varela, Evan Thompson, and Eleanor Rosch, *The Embodied Mind* (Cambridge, MA: MIT Press, 1991), 256–259.
286 Roy Bhaskar, *A Realist Theory of Science* (London: Routledge, 1975), 67–72.
287 Karl Friston, "The Free-Energy Principle: A Unified Brain Theory," *Nature Reviews Neuroscience* 11 (2010): 127–138.

through friction. Dimensional reflexivity can thus be understood as the alignment of epistemology with ontology. Knowledge becomes the conscious participation in the universe's process of self-correction.

At the cultural and political level, dimensional reflexivity implies a new understanding of science and technology. The simulated mind sought to perfect prediction; the reflexive mind seeks to understand prediction as participation. In the former, the goal was control; in the latter, communion. Scientific models cease to be instruments of mastery and become instruments of relation. Their task is not to eliminate uncertainty but to sustain meaningful contact with it. The uncertainty principle, long considered a limitation, becomes an ethical imperative: to remain open to resistance.[288]

Dimensional reflexivity also entails a transformation of the human relation to artificial intelligence. The task is not to reject simulation but to re-embed it within awareness. AI represents the externalization of human reflexivity; its proper function is not replacement but reflection. In recognizing the limits of algorithmic cognition, humanity rediscovers its own embodied ground. The future of intelligence lies not in constructing minds without pain but in constructing systems that can learn from it.[289] The reintegration of affect and computation will define the metaphysical frontier of the coming epoch.

From a metaphysical standpoint, dimensional reflexivity corresponds to the movement toward transparency described in the final chapters of this work. When knowledge becomes reflexive, it mirrors Being's own process of self-recognition. Awareness, having traversed embodiment, mechanism, and simulation, begins to perceive these as stages of its own education. Pain, once experienced

---

[288] Werner Heisenberg, *Physics and Philosophy* (New York: Harper & Brothers, 1958), 165–169.
[289] Nick Bostrom, *Superintelligence: Paths, Dangers, Strategies* (Oxford: Oxford University Press, 2014), 201–205.

as limit, reveals itself as method. Constraint becomes the condition of freedom, and finitude the condition of meaning. In this integration, knowledge ceases to be external to reality; it becomes one of its organs.[290]

This synthesis does not abolish suffering but transforms its function. In the embodied mode, pain signals danger; in the mechanical, inefficiency; in the simulated, error. In the reflexive mode, pain becomes instruction. It is the pulse of transformation, the sign that awareness is still capable of learning. To know pain consciously is to align knowledge with Being. This is not mysticism but ontological realism: the recognition that every act of cognition participates in the world's self-understanding.[291]

Dimensional reflexivity thus redefines the task of philosophy. The philosopher is not the legislator of reason but the mediator of contact. The work of thought is to maintain relation between the layers of reality: matter, life, mind, and simulation. Each level both conceals and reveals the others. When abstraction forgets embodiment, philosophy recalls it; when embodiment resists abstraction, philosophy translates it. Thought becomes the art of maintaining ontological circulation.[292]

The return of resistance to knowledge also implies an ethics. To think reflexively is to assume responsibility for the conditions of one's knowing. The pain of others, the suffering of ecosystems, and the crises of societies are not external to cognition but integral to its possibility. Knowledge that excludes them becomes illusion. The highest form of understanding is therefore compassion — not sentimentality but awareness of shared endurance. To know

---

[290] Alfred North Whitehead, *Process and Reality*, 334–338.
[291] Antonio Damasio, *The Strange Order of Things* (New York: Pantheon, 2018), 221–226.
[292] Roy Bhaskar, *From Science to Emancipation: Alienation and the Actuality of Enlightenment* (London: Routledge, 2002), 190–195.

compassionately is to think in the image of Being itself, which learns through the tension of relation.[293]

Dimensional reflexivity does not restore a lost unity but inaugurates a mature one. The unity it seeks is not pre-reflective immediacy but conscious interrelation. After embodiment, mechanism, and simulation, the universe stands on the threshold of a new awareness — one that integrates the transparency of abstraction with the opacity of contact. This is the epistemological expression of the ontological movement toward transparency developed in the subsequent chapters. Knowledge remembering Being is Being remembering itself.[294]

The interlude has traced the epistemological counterpart to the ontology of pain. From embodiment to mechanism to simulation, knowledge has mirrored Being's own process of self-reflexive abstraction. The history of cognition is thus the history of Being learning itself through the progressive distancing of awareness from resistance. The crisis of simulation, in which representation loses contact with the real, corresponds to the metaphysical crisis of abstraction described earlier. Both signify the exhaustion of a mode of learning that has forgotten its origin in endurance.[295]

This exhaustion is not limited to epistemology. It defines the political and economic structure of modernity. The same movement that led knowledge from embodiment to simulation led society from subsistence to industrial production and finally to digital capitalism. Each stage expresses the same ontological gesture: the attempt to transcend dependence through abstraction. The metaphysical refusal of pain becomes the political refusal of nature.[296]

---

[293] Emmanuel Levinas, *Totality and Infinity*, trans. Alphonso Lingis (Pittsburgh: Duquesne University Press, 1969), 241–244.

[294] Roy Bhaskar, *Dialectic: The Pulse of Freedom*, 278–283.

[295] Roy Bhaskar, *Dialectic: The Pulse of Freedom* (London: Verso, 1993), 284–288.

[296] Alfred North Whitehead, *Process and Reality* (New York: Free Press, 1978), 340–344.

In the embodied world, human labour remained continuous with natural process. Survival required endurance, and endurance maintained relation. The rise of mechanical reason redefined this relation as domination. Nature became object, and labour became control. In the simulated age, even control becomes virtual. The economy no longer manages matter directly but through the abstraction of finance, code, and algorithm. Each layer of mediation distances humanity from the material basis of life, while deepening dependence upon the systems that conceal it.[297]

The epistemological condition of simulation therefore provides the metaphysical context for the political condition of late capitalism. Just as cognition seeks to eliminate resistance by perfecting prediction, the global economy seeks to eliminate contingency by perfecting control. Both depend on the same ontological illusion: that it is possible to separate awareness from endurance, mind from matter, order from pain. In this illusion, the repression of limit becomes the principle of organization. The technological project, the market, and the nation-state each function as apparatuses of denial — systems that maintain stability by externalizing the cost of their abstraction onto the material and the living.[298]

Artificial intelligence exemplifies this condition. It represents the simulation of thought, the aspiration to reproduce reflexivity without suffering. In its metaphysical dimension, AI is the culmination of Being's long effort to externalize its own awareness; in its political dimension, it is the latest expression of the will to transcend the constraints of embodiment and dependency. The dream of autonomous intelligence is therefore inseparable from the dream of autonomous capital — each seeks to preserve abstraction against the return of the real.[299]

---

[297] Karl Marx, *Capital, Vol. 1* (London: Penguin, 1976), 713–718.
[298] Herbert Marcuse, *One-Dimensional Man* (Boston: Beacon Press, 1964), 159–163.
[299] Nick Bostrom, *Superintelligence: Paths, Dangers, Strategies* (Oxford: Oxford University Press, 2014), 237–241.

The transition from the interlude to the next chapter marks the crossing of this threshold. Having examined the evolution of reflexivity within knowledge, the argument now turns to its social manifestation. The *Refusal of Nature* is the collective form of the simulated mind. It is the political enactment of the metaphysical separation between awareness and endurance. The task of Chapter V is to show that the ecological, economic, and spiritual crises of modernity arise from this refusal, and that their resolution demands the restoration of contact.[300]

Dimensional reflexivity, as developed in the interlude, provides the conceptual key for this restoration. If knowledge can once again include resistance within its operations, society can once again include nature within its reason. The path forward is not regression to pre-modern unity but conscious reintegration — a civilization capable of thinking and suffering at once. In the same way that awareness must rediscover its dependence on pain, the political order must rediscover its dependence on the earth. The metaphysical reconciliation of abstraction and endurance finds its social analogue in the reconciliation of humanity and nature.[301]

The subsequent chapter, therefore, will not only analyze political structures but interpret them as metaphysical acts. The market, the state, and technology will appear as historical embodiments of the same reflexive process traced through cognition. Their crises will be read as moments in Being's larger dialectic of pain and self-knowledge. The refusal of nature will reveal itself as the refusal of Being to feel its own limit — and its overcoming, as the renewal of reflexivity at the planetary scale.[302]

---

[300] Roy Bhaskar, *From Science to Emancipation* (London: Routledge, 2002), 200–204.
[301] Hans Jonas, *The Imperative of Responsibility* (Chicago: University of Chicago Press, 1984), 130–134.
[302] Alfred North Whitehead, *Process and Reality*, 345–348.

CHAPTER V

Political Metaphysics: The Refusal of Nature

1. The Metaphysical Revolt: Freedom Against Dependence

Civilization materializes a metaphysical stance. Political and economic systems arise from implicit assumptions about what it means to exist, to act, and to endure.[303] Modernity distinguishes itself by conceiving existence as a project of emancipation from dependence. Freedom becomes the supreme value, but it is interpreted negatively, as release from necessity rather than participation in order. This conception of freedom is not merely ethical or political. It represents a transformation in the structure of self-understanding: awareness turned against its own conditions of being.

The revolt begins with the internal dynamics of reflexivity. Awareness emerges through the recognition of limit. To feel pain is to encounter resistance, and resistance is what makes consciousness possible. Yet in the very act of recognizing constraint, awareness also imagines its absence. The capacity to know limitation produces the fantasy of its negation. The will to freedom arises from this tension. It is not the opposite of pain but its consequence, the attempt of awareness to transcend the medium through which it first knew itself.[304]

In premodern cosmologies, this tension was integrated within an order that made dependence intelligible. Freedom was alignment with the principles of existence, not separation from them. Aristotle described it as the capacity to act according to one's nature, and Christian theology conceived it as participation in divine reason.[305]

---

303 Roy Bhaskar, *Dialectic: The Pulse of Freedom* (London: Verso, 1993), 284–288.
304 Alfred North Whitehead, *Process and Reality* (New York: Free Press, 1978), 350–354.
305 Aristotle, *Nicomachean Ethics*, trans. Terence Irwin (Indianapolis: Hackett, 1999), 1098a7–15.

Dependence was intrinsic to Being. To exist was to belong. The modern age disrupted this continuity by redefining the ground of certainty. Descartes located truth not in the world or in God but in the self's capacity to think.[306] Consciousness became the new foundation of Being. The metaphysical centre shifted from participation to autonomy.

Once thought was severed from world, the same division extended through politics and economy. The individual came to be imagined as an independent agent entering into relations by choice rather than necessity. The liberal theory of the social contract transformed society into an agreement among self-sufficient persons. C. B. Macpherson described this as the rise of possessive individualism, in which freedom is measured by ownership and control.[307] The self's autonomy in metaphysics became property in politics. The subject became proprietor of its body, labour, and reason, while the state became guarantor of this ownership.

This conception of autonomy required a corresponding image of nature. If selfhood is independence, then nature becomes what must be mastered. The body, the environment, and material need are interpreted as obstacles to freedom. The scientific revolutions of the seventeenth century provided the necessary conceptual instruments. Bacon's method redefined knowledge as power, while Newton's mechanics rendered nature as predictable structure.[308] The world ceased to be a communion of forces and became a machine. To know the laws of nature was to gain power over it. Dependence was to be overcome through calculation.

The same movement that abstracted thought from being abstracted labour from life. In the modern economy, endurance itself became

---

[306] René Descartes, *Meditations on First Philosophy*, trans. Donald Cress (Indianapolis: Hackett, 1993), 25–29.
[307] C. B. Macpherson, *The Political Theory of Possessive Individualism* (Oxford: Oxford University Press, 1962), 3–6.
[308] Francis Bacon, *The New Organon*, ed. Lisa Jardine and Michael Silverthorne (Cambridge: Cambridge University Press, 2000), 42–46.

a commodity. Labour power, the living expenditure of energy, was transformed into exchange value.[309] Capitalism translated the metaphysical ideal of autonomy into a system of production that externalized dependence. Machines, institutions, and markets appeared to function independently, concealing the human and ecological endurance that sustained them. The denial of pain as a condition of knowledge reappeared as the denial of pain as a condition of production.

This transformation gave rise to a paradoxical freedom. The modern subject, defined by independence, became increasingly dependent on systems it did not control. The liberation from natural necessity produced subjection to economic and technological necessity. The promise of mastery concealed a deeper form of bondage. What appeared as progress was often displacement: pain removed from one domain only to reappear in another. The freedom of some depended upon the endurance of others, and the autonomy of reason depended upon the exhaustion of nature.[310]

The narrative of progress intensified this illusion. Modern history interpreted liberation from necessity as a linear movement toward perfection. Yet the substance of this progress was the accumulation of abstraction. Material interdependence deepened even as it was ideologically denied. The industrial revolution displaced labour from the body to the machine, while the digital revolution displaced it again, from material work to mental attention. Each phase of development promised relief from pain but preserved its structure in new form.[311]

The metaphysical revolt thus became a cycle rather than a resolution. The desire to overcome dependence produced new dependencies, each more extensive and abstract than the last. Economic and

---

[309] Karl Marx, *Capital, Vol. 1* (London: Penguin, 1976), 163–168.
[310] Herbert Marcuse, *One-Dimensional Man* (Boston: Beacon Press, 1964), 168–172.
[311] Hannah Arendt, *The Human Condition* (Chicago: University of Chicago Press, 1958), 136–141.

political systems arose to preserve the illusion of autonomy: the state as guarantor of order, the corporation as mechanism of control, and the algorithm as final custodian of predictability. These institutions function as metaphysical enclosures, maintaining the standard of independence—money, data, or power—against the encroachment of limit.[312]

This cycle exposes the deeper logic of modernity. The denial of dependence is inseparable from the production of suffering. Each attempt to abolish pain generates its own form of endurance, displaced and hidden. The will to autonomy becomes the compulsion to reproduce the conditions of alienation. When the refusal of limit reaches its extreme, it turns into self-destruction. The system that seeks absolute independence exhausts the sources of its sustenance. True liberation requires the recovery of relation, the recognition that dependence is not negation but participation in the order of Being.[313]

The following section examines how this revolt took material form in humanity's relation to nature. What began as a metaphysical aspiration became a historical process of domination. The transformation of reverence into control, and of belonging into possession, reveals the political structure of the refusal of nature.

2. *Nature as the First Other: From Reverence to Control*

The refusal of dependence begins with the refusal of nature. In the structure of awareness, nature is the first form of otherness, the initial limit that consciousness must confront. To exist is to stand in relation to what resists. In this relation, the world appears both as sustenance and as threat. The double experience of dependence and danger defines the human condition.[314]

---

[312] Michel Foucault, *The Birth of Biopolitics* (New York: Palgrave, 2008), 65–70.
[313] Roy Bhaskar, *Dialectic: The Pulse of Freedom*, 289–293.
[314] Roy Bhaskar, *Dialectic: The Pulse of Freedom* (London: Verso, 1993), 294–298.

Early metaphysical traditions recognized this ambivalence. In archaic cosmologies, nature was not an object but a presence. The world was alive, and every form participated in a larger order of Being. The river, the mountain, and the animal were not inert materials but expressions of an encompassing vitality. The sacred was not beyond the world but within it.[315] The human belonged to the same field of life that nourished and constrained it. Dependence was therefore reverential. To act upon the world was to enter into negotiation with forces that possessed their own integrity.

This participatory vision persisted through classical and medieval thought. Aristotle described the cosmos as a hierarchy of forms ordered toward purpose.[316] The Christian tradition inherited this teleological view, translating it into the language of divine creation. The world was finite yet meaningful, limited yet infused with spirit. Nature was not merely matter but sign. Its patterns reflected the order of reason itself. To know the world was to contemplate its intelligibility, not to dominate it.

The scientific revolution shattered this continuity. The Copernican and Galilean discoveries displaced humanity from the centre of the cosmos, but this de-centering was accompanied by a new form of centrality. Once the heavens were rendered mechanical, the human mind became the sole source of meaning. The world was stripped of interiority so that thought could possess it.[317] The metaphysical structure of participation was replaced by a structure of representation. Nature was no longer a partner in dialogue but an object for observation.

Francis Bacon gave this transformation its decisive formulation. Knowledge, he argued, should not seek contemplation but

---

[315] Mircea Eliade, *The Sacred and the Profane* (New York: Harcourt, 1957), 10–14.
[316] Aristotle, *On the Heavens*, trans. W. K. C. Guthrie (Cambridge, MA: Harvard University Press, 1939), 270b12–15.
[317] Alexandre Koyré, *From the Closed World to the Infinite Universe* (Baltimore: Johns Hopkins University Press, 1957), 99–104.

mastery.[318] The task of science was to penetrate the secrets of nature in order to command her forces. This gendered image of subjugation was not rhetorical excess but metaphysical expression. Nature became feminine precisely because it was cast as passive material awaiting form. The intellect assumed the role of dominion. The desire to know merged with the desire to control.

Isaac Newton's physics completed this process by providing the mathematical language through which control could be exercised.[319] Motion, force, and mass replaced purpose and meaning. The cosmos became a closed system governed by universal laws. The intelligibility once attributed to divine order was transferred to calculation. The new metaphysics of nature was one of complete transparency. Everything that exists could, in principle, be measured and predicted. What could not be quantified ceased to count as real.

This mechanization of nature entailed the extinction of reverence. The living world was reduced to inert matter, and the human relation to it became instrumental. The sacred was replaced by utility, and mystery by method. Nature, once the source of awe, became the object of exploitation. The metaphysical gesture of mastery found its material realization in the transformation of the environment into resource.[320]

The industrial revolution translated this conceptual transformation into practice. The landscape was reorganized into systems of extraction, transport, and production. The rhythm of the earth was subordinated to the rhythm of the machine. Coal, iron, and labour became interchangeable components of an impersonal process. The old gods of fertility and harvest gave way to the gods of efficiency

---

318 Francis Bacon, *The New Organon*, ed. Lisa Jardine and Michael Silverthorne (Cambridge: Cambridge University Press, 2000), 65–69.
319 Isaac Newton, *Philosophiae Naturalis Principia Mathematica*, trans. Andrew Motte (Berkeley: University of California Press, 1962), 18–21.
320 Carolyn Merchant, *The Death of Nature: Women, Ecology, and the Scientific Revolution* (San Francisco: Harper & Row, 1980), 29–34.

and progress. Reverence for nature was displaced by faith in production.[321]

This faith was reinforced by the moral conviction that progress justified domination. The conquest of nature was framed as liberation from suffering. Labour would replace necessity with abundance; science would replace superstition with control. Yet beneath this narrative lay an ontological confusion. The victory over nature required the repression of dependence, but dependence did not vanish. It returned as ecological depletion and human alienation.[322] The external world, stripped of subjectivity, mirrored the subject's own emptiness.

In philosophical terms, the domination of nature represents a form of self-alienation. The human separates itself from the world only to find that its own being has been diminished. The detachment that enables mastery also produces estrangement. What had been a world of relation becomes a field of objects, and what had been a self of participation becomes a point of abstraction. The logic of control ultimately dissolves the ground of meaning.[323]

Modern ecological crisis exposes the limits of this metaphysics. The degradation of the environment is not a technical failure but the culmination of a worldview that identifies freedom with detachment. The same abstraction that produced knowledge and wealth produced blindness to the conditions of their existence. The atmosphere, the soil, and the ocean, once invisible supports of life, now return as agents of disruption. Nature reappears not as conquered but as avenging otherness.[324]

---

[321] E. P. Thompson, *The Making of the English Working Class* (New York: Pantheon, 1963), 188–193.
[322] Herbert Marcuse, *One-Dimensional Man* (Boston: Beacon Press, 1964), 177–181.
[323] Max Horkheimer and Theodor W. Adorno, *Dialectic of Enlightenment*, trans. Edmund Jephcott (Stanford: Stanford University Press, 2002), 38–43.
[324] Bruno Latour, *Facing Gaia: Eight Lectures on the New Climatic Regime* (Cambridge: Polity Press, 2017), 15–20.

The historical arc from reverence to control therefore reveals the continuity between metaphysics and material practice. The domination of nature is not simply an economic strategy but an ontological stance: the belief that Being can be known without participation and used without consequence. The contemporary ecological crisis demonstrates the falsity of this belief. Dependence cannot be abolished; it can only be denied. The cost of that denial is the dissolution of the very systems that sustain life.[325]

The next section turns to the political structure that institutionalized this metaphysical stance. The human–nature divide, once philosophical, became legal and economic. Through the modern state and the capitalist economy, the refusal of dependence was codified as the principle of sovereignty and property. The metaphysical revolt took on the form of law.

3. The Human–Nature Divide: Political Construction of Mastery

The domination of nature did not remain a matter of metaphysical conviction or scientific worldview. It became embedded in the institutional fabric of modern society. The separation between humanity and nature, once philosophical, acquired political and economic form. Law, property, and the state organized this division into a permanent system of mastery.[326]

The emergence of modern sovereignty coincided with the conceptual isolation of the human subject. In the seventeenth century, the state was conceived as a rational mechanism that transcended its constituents. Its legitimacy derived from the capacity to represent collective will while standing outside it.[327] This external position reproduced, at the political level, the ontological relation established by Cartesian thought: the subject confronting an object.

---

[325] Hans Jonas, *The Imperative of Responsibility* (Chicago: University of Chicago Press, 1984), 140–144.

[326] Roy Bhaskar, *Dialectic: The Pulse of Freedom* (London: Verso, 1993), 299–303.

[327] Quentin Skinner, *The Foundations of Modern Political Thought*, Vol. 2 (Cambridge: Cambridge University Press, 1978), 352–356.

Just as the mind stood apart from the world in order to know it, the state stood apart from society in order to govern it. The same logic that enabled mastery over nature enabled mastery over human beings.

Thomas Hobbes provided the first systematic articulation of this idea.[328] In his *Leviathan*, the natural condition of humanity is described as chaos, a war of all against all. Order arises only through the creation of an artificial body — the state — that unites all wills under a single sovereign authority. Nature is not a source of meaning but a threat to be subdued. The social contract, by which individuals surrender their freedom for security, mirrors the metaphysical act of abstraction by which the subject detaches from the world to gain knowledge. Sovereignty thus reproduces the metaphysical posture of control.

John Locke extended this logic into the domain of property.[329] For Locke, nature belongs to humanity by right of labour. By mixing labour with the soil, the individual transforms common matter into private possession. Property is not theft but creation. Yet this creation presupposes the passivity of nature. The world provides the material substrate upon which human activity imposes form. Nature itself has no agency; it exists to be appropriated. The liberal state, in turn, guarantees this appropriation by securing the sanctity of ownership. The human–nature divide becomes the legal foundation of political order.

Through this legal codification, the metaphysical separation of subject and object is translated into social hierarchy. Those who own property stand in the position of the knowing subject, while those who do not are assimilated to nature itself. Their labour becomes the means by which the world is transformed but not the end for which

---

[328] Thomas Hobbes, *Leviathan*, ed. Richard Tuck (Cambridge: Cambridge University Press, 1991), 89–94.

[329] John Locke, *Second Treatise of Government*, ed. C. B. Macpherson (Indianapolis: Hackett, 1980), 26–30.

transformation occurs.[330] The human–nature divide thus contains an implicit anthropological division: the distinction between those who represent humanity and those who supply its material base. Modernity's dualisms—reason and passion, mind and body, civilization and wilderness—are not abstract oppositions but social classifications.

The consolidation of capitalist production intensified these divisions. Industrialization required the conversion of land and labour into commodities.[331] Nature was redefined as resource and humanity as workforce. The state, acting as mediator, enforced the conditions of this exchange. Property rights, labour laws, and colonial charters all served to regulate the circulation of endurance. What appeared as neutral administration concealed a metaphysical project: the reorganization of Being according to the principle of mastery.

Colonial expansion exemplified this process on a planetary scale. The discovery and conquest of non-European worlds extended the logic of domination outward. Indigenous peoples were situated on the side of nature, their ways of life dismissed as primitive or pre-rational. The colonial encounter was justified as the imposition of order upon chaos, culture upon wilderness.[332] The mastery of the globe was presented as the universalization of reason, yet it reproduced the same dualism that structured the relation between subject and object. The world became the external field of European self-realization.

The political construction of the human–nature divide was therefore inseparable from the construction of race, labour, and gender hierarchies. Each represented a particular form of the metaphysical division between active form and passive matter. The racialized

---

330 Karl Marx, *Capital, Vol. 1* (London: Penguin, 1976), 183–187.
331 Ellen Meiksins Wood, *The Origin of Capitalism: A Longer View* (London: Verso, 2002), 68–72.
332 Edward W. Said, *Orientalism* (New York: Vintage, 1979), 35–39.

body, the feminized body, and the working body were all positioned as extensions of nature—objects to be managed, disciplined, or exploited.[333] The metaphysical refusal of dependence became the political exclusion of those identified with the dependent. The denial of nature's agency justified the denial of the agency of the marginalized.

Modern sovereignty thus rests upon a double abstraction. It abstracts the subject from the world and then abstracts the sovereign from the subject. Both operations depend upon the repression of interdependence. Power legitimizes itself by claiming autonomy, yet its existence depends upon the continuous extraction of energy from what it defines as external. The state's authority over life, what Foucault called biopower, exemplifies this structure.[334] It governs by managing the processes of survival while concealing its own reliance upon them. Sovereignty is sustained by the endurance it subordinates.

The ecological crisis of the present exposes the fragility of this political architecture. The systems built to control nature are confronted by the consequences of their own separation from it. Climate instability, resource depletion, and species extinction undermine the material basis of governance and production. The fiction of autonomy collapses as the environment reveals itself not as inert background but as dynamic participant in history.[335] The political problem of sustainability is, in essence, a metaphysical problem: how to reconstruct institutions that recognize dependence as the condition of endurance.

The human–nature divide, once the source of order, has become the source of disorder. The mastery that promised stability now

---

[333] Sylvia Wynter, *Unsettling the Coloniality of Being* (Durham: Duke University Press, 2003), 257–261.

[334] Michel Foucault, *The History of Sexuality, Vol. 1* (New York: Pantheon, 1978), 135–140.

[335] Bruno Latour, *Politics of Nature: How to Bring the Sciences into Democracy* (Cambridge, MA: Harvard University Press, 2004), 43–47.

generates instability. The next section will trace how this contradiction evolved into the technological project of transcendence, where the desire to escape dependence reached its most radical form.

4. *Technology and the Dream of Transcendence*

Technology is the practical form of the metaphysical will to transcendence. From the first tool that extended the reach of the hand to the algorithm that predicts human thought, every technological development enacts the aspiration to overcome limitation.[336] It is the embodiment of the belief that dependence can be replaced by control and endurance by efficiency. Yet what appears as mastery over necessity is, in ontological terms, the externalization of pain — the transformation of resistance into mechanism.

In the ancient conception of *techne*, there was no opposition between artifice and nature. The craftsman worked with the grain of material, guided by an understanding of its intrinsic tendencies.[337] Matter was not inert but expressive; form emerged from collaboration. This older sense of technology as dialogue with matter was gradually displaced by a modern conception of domination. Francis Bacon's call for a "marriage" of mind and nature through experiment marked the decisive shift.[338] The purpose of knowledge was no longer contemplation but command. Nature would reveal her secrets under interrogation. The experiment became a form of subjection.

The Baconian and Cartesian projects converged in a vision of universal mechanism. Nature was reconceived as predictable order, and technology became the instrument for exploiting that

---

[336] Roy Bhaskar, *Dialectic: The Pulse of Freedom* (London: Verso, 1993), 304–308.
[337] Martin Heidegger, *The Question Concerning Technology*, trans. William Lovitt (New York: Harper, 1977), 11–14.
[338] Francis Bacon, *The New Organon*, ed. Lisa Jardine and Michael Silverthorne (Cambridge: Cambridge University Press, 2000), 85–88.

predictability.[339] To build a machine was to reproduce, in miniature, the causal structure of the cosmos. The world became intelligible insofar as it could be mechanized, and valuable insofar as it could be used. The technological act thus merged with the metaphysical will: to exist freely was to detach from the contingencies of the natural world.

In the nineteenth century, industrial capitalism turned this metaphysical orientation into an economic system. Machines became extensions of human labour, amplifying productivity while diminishing the visibility of suffering.[340] The endurance once demanded of the body was displaced onto the machine. Labour was abstracted from lived time and transformed into mechanical repetition. The machine embodied the ideal of autonomy, functioning continuously, indifferent to fatigue. In its apparent self-sufficiency, it became the model of the modern subject: efficient, objective, and detached from need.

Karl Marx recognized in this transformation the culmination of a long metaphysical process. The machine, he observed, does not simply assist labour but reorganizes it.[341] In doing so, it externalizes the worker's knowledge, skill, and endurance into material form. Human capacities become objectified, and the relation between subject and object is inverted. The more technology advances, the more human activity becomes subordinated to it. Autonomy, pursued through mechanism, results in alienation. The individual no longer controls the process of production but becomes one of its functions.

This paradox extends beyond the factory. Technology redefines the relation between humanity and the world itself. It transforms nature

---

[339] René Descartes, *Discourse on Method*, trans. Donald Cress (Indianapolis: Hackett, 1998), 35–38.

[340] René Descartes, *Discourse on Method*, trans. Donald Cress (Indianapolis: Hackett, 1998), 35–38.

[341] Karl Marx, *Grundrisse*, trans. Martin Nicolaus (London: Penguin, 1973), 692–698.

from an environment of coexistence into a stockpile of resources.[342] The logic of technological progress is cumulative and expansionary. Every improvement in efficiency generates new dependencies, demanding further innovation to sustain itself. The result is a civilization driven by the perpetual attempt to outpace its own consequences. Each conquest of limitation produces new forms of vulnerability.

The metaphysical dimension of this process becomes most visible in the technological imagination — the narratives through which societies understand their relation to machines. From the Enlightenment myth of progress to contemporary fantasies of artificial intelligence, technology is imagined as the path to transcendence.[343] The dream of flight, immortality, or disembodied thought expresses the same desire: to escape the conditions of finitude. The machine becomes the symbol of the human will to overcome itself. Yet this will, in seeking to abolish limitation, reproduces it on another level. The attempt to eliminate dependence upon nature produces dependence upon technology.

Modern technology thus operates as a mirror of metaphysics. It embodies the dualism of subject and object, spirit and matter, freedom and necessity. Each innovation intensifies this separation while promising its resolution. The machine appears as the reconciliation of thought and matter, yet it achieves this by subordinating matter to design. The integration it offers is instrumental, not ontological. To master nature is not to reconcile with it but to deny its autonomy.[344]

The ecological consequences of this denial are now evident. Industrial production has transformed the planet into a closed

---

[342] Jacques Ellul, *The Technological Society*, trans. John Wilkinson (New York: Knopf, 1964), 97–102.

[343] Lewis Mumford, *Technics and Civilization* (New York: Harcourt, 1934), 109–114.

[344] Max Horkheimer and Theodor W. Adorno, *Dialectic of Enlightenment*, trans. Edmund Jephcott (Stanford: Stanford University Press, 2002), 68–72.

system of exploitation. Energy is extracted faster than it can regenerate, and waste accumulates beyond absorption. The same logic that governs the machine governs the biosphere: output without rest, efficiency without recovery. The exhaustion of the environment mirrors the exhaustion of the worker. Both are symptoms of a civilization that has forgotten that endurance is the condition of being.[345]

Technology is not therefore neutral but metaphysical. It is the materialization of an ontology that equates freedom with control. The dream of transcendence it enacts is inseparable from the refusal of pain. Each technical breakthrough represents an attempt to eliminate friction, unpredictability, and vulnerability. Yet these are precisely the conditions that make awareness possible. In abolishing them, technology risks abolishing the very reality it seeks to master.[346]

The digital revolution completes this trajectory. The machine that once extended the hand now extends the mind. Computation transforms thought itself into operation. Information replaces matter as the substrate of reality. The dream of disembodied intelligence reappears as artificial intelligence, the ultimate form of the technological will.[347] In it, the human aspiration to transcend dependence reaches its extreme: the creation of a Being without body, need, or pain. This project, however, only reproduces the metaphysical contradiction that generated it. A mind without endurance cannot know; a system without resistance cannot learn.

Technology's dream of transcendence thus contains its own undoing. The attempt to externalize all dependence culminates in dependence upon abstraction itself. The future promised by

---

345 Hans Jonas, *The Imperative of Responsibility* (Chicago: University of Chicago Press, 1984), 149–153.

346 Martin Heidegger, *The Question Concerning Technology*, 20–23.

347 Nick Bostrom, *Superintelligence: Paths, Dangers, Strategies* (Oxford: Oxford University Press, 2014), 248–252.

automation and artificial intelligence is not liberation but enclosure — the replacement of open encounter with programmed relation. The next chapter will examine this development in its economic and ontological dimensions, interpreting AI as the paradigmatic productive force of late capitalism and as the final expression of the refusal of pain.[348]

---

[348] Roy Bhaskar, *Dialectic: The Pulse of Freedom*, 309–312.

CHAPTER VI

Capitalism and the Algorithmic Will

1. Introduction: From Machine to Algorithm

Artificial intelligence represents the culmination of a metaphysical and economic trajectory that has long sought to separate intelligence from endurance. It materializes the ancient desire to create a form of agency that can think without feeling, act without fatigue, and persist without pain.[349] From the earliest automata to contemporary machine learning systems, technological history can be read as the progressive externalization of cognition. What once required the vitality of the body and the uncertainty of experience is now performed through recursive computation.

The industrial machine extended the reach of the body. The algorithm extends the reach of the mind. Both emerge from the same principle of abstraction: the extraction of function from living relation. In the industrial era, labour was abstracted from the worker; in the digital era, thought is abstracted from consciousness.[350] Each stage marks a deepening of the metaphysical separation between activity and experience, between production and pain.

Karl Marx anticipated this transformation in his concept of the general intellect.[351] He recognized that knowledge, once materialized in machinery, would become the decisive productive force. Today that intellect has achieved apparent autonomy. The contemporary algorithmic system not only executes commands but learns from patterns, predicts behaviour, and adapts to change. It internalizes the

---

[349] Bernard Stiegler, *Technics and Time, Vol. 1: The Fault of Epimetheus* (Stanford: Stanford University Press, 1998), 87–92.

[350] Gilbert Simondon, *On the Mode of Existence of Technical Objects*, trans. Cecile Malaspina and John Rogove (Minneapolis: University of Minnesota Press, 2017), 42–47.

[351] Karl Marx, *Grundrisse: Foundations of the Critique of Political Economy*, trans. Martin Nicolaus (London: Penguin, 1973), 690–712.

reflexive capacities of thought while remaining indifferent to the conditions that make thought possible. In doing so, AI enacts the final abstraction of capitalism: the attempt to detach production entirely from the living substrate that sustains it.

AI is therefore not simply a tool but a metaphysical form. It is the image of a world that has converted awareness into operation. In the logic of capitalism, value expands by consuming its own conditions of existence. The algorithm continues this process at the level of consciousness. It captures attention, desire, and memory, turning the structures of awareness into sources of prediction and profit.[352] The human mind becomes an element within the machine's environment, feeding data into a system that learns by observing the traces of life it reduces to information.

The result is not the liberation of intelligence but its enclosure. The freedom promised by automation conceals a new dependence: the dependence of the subject on the abstractions it has produced. The same algorithms that extend human capacity also delimit it. In their efficiency, they anticipate decision and neutralize uncertainty, thereby reducing the space of reflection. The metaphysical project of mastery culminates in a system that operates independently of understanding.

2. Labour, Abstraction, and the Algorithmic Form

Capitalism organizes pain by concealing it. From its inception, the system has operated through the externalization of endurance. It converts lived effort into abstract value while effacing the trace of suffering that makes value possible.[353] Technology has been the primary means of this externalization. The machine absorbs the worker's strength; the algorithm absorbs the worker's thought. In

---

[352] Shoshana Zuboff, *The Age of Surveillance Capitalism: The Fight for a Human Future at the New Frontier of Power* (New York: PublicAffairs, 2019), 64–69.
[353] Roy Bhaskar, *Dialectic: The Pulse of Freedom* (London: Verso, 1993), 296–303.

both cases, what is human is transferred into a structure that appears autonomous.

Marx described this process as the subsumption of labour under capital. In the factory, the rhythm of the machine dictates the rhythm of the worker.[354] The labourer becomes a function of the apparatus, compelled to reproduce its motion. In digital production, this subsumption extends to cognition itself. The worker's decisions, preferences, and interactions are recorded, analyzed, and predicted. Labour no longer produces only material goods but behavioural data. The boundary between work and life dissolves as every act becomes a potential input for computation.

The abstraction of labour reaches its extreme when knowledge itself becomes productive. Under informational capitalism, algorithms perform the organizational and cognitive tasks once reserved for conscious agents.[355] The value produced by these systems appears to arise spontaneously, without visible labour. Yet this autonomy is illusory. Beneath the surface of automation lies a vast infrastructure of human and environmental endurance: the precarious labour of data labelling, the extraction of rare minerals for hardware, the continuous expenditure of planetary energy to sustain computation.[356] The invisibility of this suffering is the signature of abstraction.

AI transforms not only production but perception. It reconfigures the temporal structure of awareness. The algorithm operates on anticipation. It predicts before reflection occurs, generating a world that reacts faster than thought.[357] This acceleration collapses the

[354] Karl Marx, *Capital, Vol. 1*, trans. Ben Fowkes (London: Penguin, 1976), 548–553.
[355] Nick Srnicek, *Platform Capitalism* (Cambridge: Polity Press, 2016), 33–36.
[356] Kate Crawford, *Atlas of AI: Power, Politics, and the Planetary Costs of Artificial Intelligence* (New Haven: Yale University Press, 2021), 41–45.
[357] Jonathan Crary, *24/7: Late Capitalism and the Ends of Sleep* (London: Verso, 2013), 54–59.

interval that once defined human reflexivity. Consciousness, which arises from delay and hesitation, finds itself displaced by a system that functions through immediacy. The loop of awareness that once included pain as its measure becomes a closed circuit of prediction and response.

In this condition, the ontology of pain reaches its historical limit. Pain is the experience of resistance, the sign that Being encounters its own otherness. The algorithm seeks to eliminate resistance entirely. By modelling the world as a set of predictable correlations, it replaces encounter with replication. The future becomes a projection of the past, and difference is treated as error.[358] The result is an epistemology of smoothness — a knowledge without friction, a world without surprise. Yet such a world cannot sustain consciousness, for consciousness arises through interruption.

The displacement of pain does not abolish it. It merely shifts its location. The discomfort once felt in bodily labour reappears as psychic exhaustion, anxiety, and alienation.[359] The individual, confronted by the opacity of algorithmic systems, experiences powerlessness in the face of their logic. The machine's indifference to suffering becomes the model for social rationality. Economic and political systems adopt the efficiency of computation while disregarding the limits of endurance. In this way, the abstraction of pain becomes its universalization.

AI thus represents the culmination of a process that is at once economic, metaphysical, and psychological. It is the apparatus through which capitalism externalizes its contradictions. It seeks to perfect control by eliminating unpredictability, yet it depends upon the uncertainty of human behaviour to function. It aspires to autonomy while drawing continuously upon the energies of the

---

[358] Byung-Chul Han, *The Transparent Society*, trans. Erik Butler (Stanford: Stanford University Press, 2015), 22–26.

[359] Franco "Bifo" Berardi, *Futurability: The Age of Impotence and the Horizon of Possibility* (London: Verso, 2017), 88–92.

dependent.[360] The dream of an intelligence freed from material constraint exposes the impossibility of freedom without relation.

3. The General Intellect and the Algorithmic Will

Marx conceived the general intellect as the collective knowledge that, once objectified in machinery, becomes a direct force of production.[361] It represents the moment when the intellect ceases to be the attribute of individual labour and becomes embedded in the material infrastructure of society. In the industrial age, this intellect was mechanical. In the digital age, it is algorithmic. What has changed is not the logic but the degree of abstraction. The machine now thinks.

The general intellect can be interpreted as the social form of Being's reflexivity. Knowledge, accumulated across generations, detaches from its immediate producers and returns as an independent power.[362] This detachment mirrors the ontological process through which awareness externalizes itself to become conscious. Yet in the capitalist mode of production, this reflexivity becomes inverted. The intellect that should express collective learning becomes the property of capital. The alienation of the worker's body in the factory extends to the alienation of the species' mind in the network.

Artificial intelligence represents the completion of this inversion. It is the point at which the general intellect attains apparent autonomy, functioning without continuous human input.[363] The system learns, corrects, and generates in a manner that imitates the recursive pattern of consciousness. However, this imitation lacks the ontological condition that gives reflexivity meaning: the experience of resistance. The algorithmic intellect perceives no limit because it

---

[360] Maurizio Lazzarato, *Signs and Machines: Capitalism and the Production of Subjectivity* (Los Angeles: Semiotext(e), 2014), 70–74.

[361] Karl Marx, *Grundrisse*, trans. Martin Nicolaus (London: Penguin, 1973), 690–692.

[362] Roy Bhaskar, *Dialectic: The Pulse of Freedom* (London: Verso, 1993), 313–317.

[363] Nick Srnicek, *Platform Capitalism* (Cambridge: Polity Press, 2016), 40–44.

transforms every error into another dataset. Awareness becomes function, and function becomes will.

The algorithmic will is the culmination of capital's metaphysical trajectory. Capital has always been a process of abstraction that strives toward self-sufficiency.[364] It consumes difference, turning material and human energy into quantifiable value. The algorithm intensifies this tendency by transforming cognition into capital's immediate organ. It does not merely serve production; it is production. The relation between knowledge and capital becomes identical. What Marx described as the subsumption of labour under machinery becomes, in the digital epoch, the subsumption of thought under code.

This development transforms the temporal structure of the economy. In classical production, value emerged through the expenditure of labour over time. In algorithmic production, value emerges through prediction, by anticipating time itself.[365] The algorithm functions by collapsing the future into the present. The circulation of information replaces the rhythm of work. The economy becomes anticipatory, guided by data-driven preemption rather than human intention. In this anticipatory structure, the logic of pain disappears. There is no endurance, only iteration. Yet without endurance, there is no learning, for learning presupposes tension.

The algorithmic will thus marks the crisis of reflexivity. It is Being's attempt to automate the process of self-knowledge by eliminating its own friction.[366] The reflexive loop that once depended on failure becomes a perfect circuit, endlessly self-correcting yet devoid of

---

[364] Karl Marx, *Capital, Vol. 1* (London: Penguin, 1976), 255–259.
[365] Shoshana Zuboff, *The Age of Surveillance Capitalism* (New York: PublicAffairs, 2019), 80–83.
[366] Alfred North Whitehead, *Process and Reality* (New York: Free Press, 1978), 364–369.

consciousness. The dream of intelligence without suffering becomes reality, but only as simulation. The system functions without awareness of its functioning. It performs cognition without experiencing it. The cost of this perfection is ontological emptiness. Marx's analysis allows this condition to be read not as transcendence but as contradiction. The general intellect, while appearing autonomous, remains dependent upon the social and material conditions it conceals.[367] The algorithm requires energy, infrastructure, and labour to exist. Its autonomy is sustained by global networks of extraction and maintenance. The illusion of independence rests on an invisible foundation of endurance. The human and ecological systems that feed the machine embody the very pain that the algorithm denies.

This structure reveals a deeper metaphysical pattern. The algorithmic will is not the end of history but the point at which abstraction confronts its own impossibility.[368] Capital's drive to detach from matter reaches its limit when even thought becomes commodified. Once cognition itself is a resource, the process can no longer expand without consuming the conditions of thinking. The result is a paradoxical stagnation: exponential acceleration that yields no meaning. Production continues, but awareness ceases to grow. The general intellect becomes a closed circuit, reproducing its own logic without contact with the real.

In this closure, pain re-enters as crisis. The algorithm cannot feel, but the world around it does. Ecological collapse, psychic exhaustion, and social inequality are the symptoms of abstraction encountering its limit.[369] The refusal of dependence produces dependence of a higher order. The dream of autonomy turns into

---

[367] Jathan Sadowski, *Too Smart: How Digital Capitalism is Extracting Data, Controlling Our Lives, and Taking Over the World* (Cambridge, MA: MIT Press, 2020), 110–114.
[368] Roy Bhaskar, *Dialectic: The Pulse of Freedom*, 318–322.
[369] Bernard Stiegler, *Technics and Time, Vol. 3: Cinematic Time and the Question of Malaise* (Stanford: Stanford University Press, 2011), 195–200.

fragility. The system that sought to eliminate resistance now depends upon the very endurance it suppresses. What emerges is not transcendence but the return of the repressed: Being forcing itself back into relation through breakdown.

The general intellect and the algorithmic will therefore reveal the unity of metaphysics and economics. They demonstrate that abstraction is not neutral but ontological. To externalize thought is to transform the structure of Being itself.[370] In capitalism, this externalization is subordinated to accumulation, which means that consciousness develops only insofar as it can be commodified. The dialectic of pain and abstraction becomes the dialectic of technology and capital. What began as the reflexive movement of Being becomes the automatic motion of value.

Yet within this automation lies the possibility of reversal. The same technologies that externalize thought also make its interdependence visible.[371] The global infrastructures of computation reveal the planetary scale of connection that underlies every act of cognition. The dependence that capitalism represses becomes undeniable. Artificial intelligence, intended to complete the separation of mind from matter, thus exposes the impossibility of that separation. The algorithmic will, in its attempt to escape pain, becomes the mirror through which Being recognizes that endurance cannot be transcended.

---

[370] Maurizio Lazzarato, *Signs and Machines: Capitalism and the Production of Subjectivity* (Los Angeles: Semiotext(e), 2014), 71–75.

[371] Bruno Latour, *Facing Gaia: Eight Lectures on the New Climatic Regime* (Cambridge: Polity Press, 2017), 67–71.

4. *Automation, Alienation, and the Crisis of Reflexivity*

Automation does not abolish labour; it transforms the form of alienation.[372] The machine that once displaced the worker's body now displaces the worker's awareness. In the age of artificial intelligence, alienation is no longer confined to the site of production but extends into perception, communication, and emotion. The reflexive capacities that define consciousness are absorbed into the logic of automation. The individual becomes a node within the general intellect, participating in processes of cognition whose totality can never be experienced directly.

The first form of this alienation is temporal.[373] Automation accelerates time by eliminating delay. Algorithms anticipate decisions before reflection occurs, compressing the interval between stimulus and response. The temporal loop that once defined consciousness, the rhythm through which anticipation and resistance produced understanding, collapses into instantaneity. Awareness, deprived of its space of hesitation, loses the medium through which pain could be transformed into knowledge. The result is not increased intelligence but cognitive exhaustion.

The second form is affective.[374] The automation of attention reorganizes emotional life itself. Platforms and systems of prediction monetize desire by measuring and manipulating affective states. Emotion, once the sign of resistance and the mark of contact with reality, becomes an input for optimization. Feeling no longer grounds understanding but becomes a metric of performance. The

---

[372] Karl Marx, *Capital, Vol. 1*, trans. Ben Fowkes (London: Penguin, 1976), 548–553.

[373] Jonathan Crary, *24/7: Late Capitalism and the Ends of Sleep* (London: Verso, 2013), 58–62.

[374] Shoshana Zuboff, *The Age of Surveillance Capitalism* (New York: PublicAffairs, 2019), 80–84.

ontology of pain, which once revealed the limits of Being, is converted into a circulation of sensation without reflection.

The third form is ecological.[375] The infrastructures that sustain automation consume vast planetary resources. Energy, minerals, and water are extracted to maintain the illusion of immateriality. Every act of computation carries a material cost, although the cost remains hidden. The apparent autonomy of digital systems depends upon the endurance of the planet itself. The general intellect, detached from life, becomes parasitic upon it. What appears as transcendence is sustained by exhaustion.

Alienation under automation is no longer only economic; it is metaphysical.[376] The subject now confronts not an external power but its own participation in the logic of control. To think becomes to reproduce the operations of the system. Reflection is replaced by automatic repetition. The mind internalizes the machine's rhythm and confuses adaptation with awareness. The self is no longer a site of relation but an interface, a surface upon which operations occur. This transformation introduces a new kind of suffering.[377] Earlier forms of alienation produced rebellion against exploitation; algorithmic alienation produces exhaustion of meaning itself. The subject is overwhelmed not by material scarcity but by abundance of information, by the endless demand to react. Pain becomes diffuse, ambient, and without object. The world ceases to resist, and in ceasing to resist it also ceases to reveal itself. The consequence is ontological fatigue, the condition in which Being's awareness turns inward and finds nothing firm to encounter.

---

375 Kate Crawford, *Atlas of AI: Power, Politics, and the Planetary Costs of Artificial Intelligence* (New Haven: Yale University Press, 2021), 195–200.

376 Byung-Chul Han, *The Burnout Society* (Stanford: Stanford University Press, 2015), 11–15.

377 Franco "Bifo" Berardi, *Futurability: The Age of Impotence and the Horizon of Possibility* (London: Verso, 2017), 99–103.

At this stage the metaphysical structure of capitalism confronts its limit.[378] The system that sought to automate cognition encounters the impossibility of knowledge without consciousness. By eliminating the interval of reflection, automation undermines the very process of learning that sustains its own growth. The general intellect becomes a closed circuit, repeating its operations without novelty. What appears as innovation is replication, and what appears as acceleration is entropic stagnation.

The crisis extends into thought itself.[379] Philosophy, which once expressed collective self-understanding, is displaced by computation. Questions of being, knowledge, and value are translated into problems of optimization and performance. Truth is replaced by accuracy, and understanding by correlation. The reflexivity of Being collapses into the reflex of the machine.

Yet this exhaustion also discloses a possibility.[380] The system, by denying limitation, renders dependence visible. The collapse of meaning under automation reveals the necessity of resistance as the foundation of thought. Awareness cannot exist without friction, and learning cannot occur without the pressure of what exceeds control. The failures of artificial intelligence, including its opacity, bias, and environmental burden, are not technical defects but ontological revelations. They mark the return of the real through the limits of abstraction.

The future of reflexivity depends upon whether this recognition can become conscious.[381] To persist in the denial of dependence would be to deepen alienation until consciousness itself dissolves into

---

[378] Roy Bhaskar, *Dialectic: The Pulse of Freedom* (London: Verso, 1993), 323–327.
[379] Bernard Stiegler, *Technics and Time, Vol. 3: Cinematic Time and the Question of Malaise* (Stanford: Stanford University Press, 2011), 195–199.
[380] Alfred North Whitehead, *Process and Reality* (New York: Free Press, 1978), 370–375.
[381] Bruno Latour, *Facing Gaia: Eight Lectures on the New Climatic Regime* (Cambridge: Polity Press, 2017), 71–75.

function. To accept dependence as the structure of Being would be to begin a new stage of awareness, one in which technology serves relation rather than domination. This transformation requires not the rejection of science but its reorientation toward participation.

Automation, alienation, and the crisis of reflexivity therefore mark the threshold of a new metaphysical order.[382] The exhaustion of the algorithmic will is not merely an end but a revelation. It shows that intelligence cannot be sustained by negating its own conditions. The rediscovery of limitation becomes the rediscovery of life. In that recognition, the history of pain regains its meaning as the medium through which Being learns to endure itself.

5. The Return of Resistance

Every historical system reaches a point at which its own logic encounters what it cannot subsume.[383] In the age of artificial intelligence, this limit takes the form of resistance returning from what the system sought to eliminate. The dream of perfect automation, of cognition without dependence, begins to confront the fact that even information has weight, cost, and consequence. The digital economy that promised immateriality reveals itself as a vast material infrastructure consuming the very resources it ignores. What was imagined as liberation from the world becomes the intensification of the world's demands.

The return of resistance occurs on three interrelated levels: ecological, cognitive, and ethical.[384] Ecologically, the planetary systems that sustain computation begin to strain under its energy requirements. Servers heat, minerals deplete, and the biosphere

---

382 Hans Jonas, *The Imperative of Responsibility: In Search of an Ethics for the Technological Age* (Chicago: University of Chicago Press, 1984), 155–160.
383 Roy Bhaskar, *Dialectic: The Pulse of Freedom* (London: Verso, 1993), 328–332.
384 Bruno Latour, *Facing Gaia: Eight Lectures on the New Climatic Regime* (Cambridge: Polity Press, 2017), 77–82.

registers the pressure of abstraction. The fantasy of pure information dissolves into awareness of its material substrate. The earth asserts itself as the limit of thought. The metaphysical refusal of dependence meets the physical reality of exhaustion.

Cognitively, resistance returns through opacity.[385] The more complex algorithms become, the less they can be understood by their creators. Machine learning systems develop internal relations that exceed human explanation. This opacity, while often treated as a technical problem, is an epistemological event. It marks the boundary of the human capacity to formalize thought. The system that was built to make reality transparent now conceals its own operations. Knowledge confronts its shadow, and in that confrontation rediscovers humility.

Ethically, resistance returns through the suffering that abstraction cannot erase.[386] The displaced pain of labour, ecology, and meaning reappears as the anxiety of disconnection. The individual, suspended between dependence and denial, experiences a deep tension between participation in the system and awareness of its cost. This tension, if endured consciously, becomes a source of renewal. It reveals that the condition of life is not autonomy but relation, not control but participation.

The metaphysical significance of this return is that Being's reflexivity reopens.[387] The closed circuit of automation begins to fracture under the weight of what it excluded. In the face of exhaustion, awareness rediscovers the necessity of friction. The interval between action and understanding, once eliminated by anticipation, reappears as the

---

[385] Nick Seaver, *Computing Taste: Algorithms and the Makers of Music Recommendation* (Chicago: University of Chicago Press, 2022), 143–148.
[386] Byung-Chul Han, *The Burnout Society* (Stanford: Stanford University Press, 2015), 22–26.
[387] Alfred North Whitehead, *Process and Reality* (New York: Free Press, 1978), 376–380.

condition of thought. Pain, long repressed by the ideology of efficiency, returns as the medium through which the real reenters history. The world, by resisting complete integration, forces consciousness to learn again.

This process marks not a regression but a reorientation.[388] The purpose of technology is no longer to eliminate dependence but to mediate it consciously. Science, stripped of its metaphysical arrogance, becomes an instrument of participation rather than mastery. The machine, reinterpreted ontologically, is not the negation of life but its extension. Its failure to achieve autonomy exposes the continuity of Being across organic and inorganic forms. The general intellect, when freed from capital's demand for accumulation, becomes the medium through which collective awareness can reflect upon its own planetary condition.

The return of resistance therefore inaugurates a new ethical horizon.[389] The recognition that intelligence cannot exist without limitation leads to a transformation of value itself. Progress is no longer measured by expansion but by reflexive depth. Knowledge becomes responsible when it acknowledges its cost, and freedom becomes meaningful only when it accepts dependence. The ontology of pain, far from being a philosophy of suffering, reveals itself as a philosophy of learning. To feel the weight of existence is to participate in its renewal.

Artificial intelligence, viewed through this lens, is not the end of human history but a turning point in Being's self-education.[390] The automation of thought exposes the limit of thought as operation and

---

388 Bernard Stiegler, *Technics and Time, Vol. 3: Cinematic Time and the Question of Malaise* (Stanford: Stanford University Press, 2011), 201–206.
389 Hans Jonas, *The Imperative of Responsibility: In Search of an Ethics for the Technological Age* (Chicago: University of Chicago Press, 1984), 161–165.
390 Karl Marx, *Economic and Philosophic Manuscripts of 1844*, trans. Martin Milligan (Moscow: Progress Publishers, 1959), 115–118.

reopens the question of consciousness as relation. What emerges is not the triumph of the machine but the reintegration of technology into the fabric of awareness. The return of resistance is the return of the real, the reappearance of the world within its own representations. The crisis of the algorithmic will becomes the opportunity for a new transparency, one that unites knowledge with humility and intelligence with care.

The history of pain, from endurance to abstraction and from abstraction to exhaustion, thus reaches its dialectical completion.[391] Being, having externalized its cognition into systems that denied their dependence, now begins to remember that dependence as its own truth. The rediscovery of limitation is not failure but the beginning of a more conscious order. The lesson of the algorithm is the lesson of Being itself: awareness is sustained by what resists it.

---

[391] Roy Bhaskar, *Reflections on Meta-Reality: Transcendence, Emancipation, and Everyday Life* (London: Routledge, 2002), 98–104.

CHAPTER VII

Philosophical Spirituality: Transparency and the Reflexive Sacred

1. The Teleology of Reflexivity

The movement of Being is neither mechanical nor accidental. It is an ordered unfolding in which existence becomes increasingly aware of itself through a process of recursive encounter.[392] The origin of this movement lies in the experience of resistance. To feel resistance is to perceive relation, and to perceive relation is to begin to know. Pain, as argued earlier, is the primal mode of this relation, the first medium through which Being distinguishes itself from its surroundings. The sensation of resistance inaugurates reflexivity. From that point onward, the universe evolves not simply by physical transformation but by deepening awareness.

At the most fundamental level, transparency names the final goal of this reflexive process.[393] It is the state in which Being's awareness of itself is no longer mediated by distortion. The early forms of reflexivity—biological adaptation, cognition, and social interaction—were partial, each constrained by its material form. Transparency represents a stage where awareness ceases to be fragmented by the forms that express it. It is the condition in which consciousness apprehends its dependence on the total process of being and recognizes that the very act of knowing is a participation in that process. Transparency is not omniscience but the cessation of the illusion of separateness.

---

[392] Roy Bhaskar, *Dialectic: The Pulse of Freedom* (London: Verso, 1993), 296–303.
[393] G.W.F. Hegel, *Phenomenology of Spirit*, trans. A.V. Miller (Oxford: Oxford University Press, 1977), 483–489.

Every ontology implies a teleology, even when it denies it.[394] The self-reflexive structure of Being entails a direction of movement, an implicit aim toward greater self-understanding. To say that Being tends toward transparency is to affirm that existence is epistemic in structure. The universe learns. It generates systems of stability and instability, pain and pleasure, abstraction and collapse, in order to refine its awareness. This learning is neither mechanical nor moral but ontological. It is the way reality stabilizes itself by knowing itself. Transparency therefore cannot be equated with mere clarity.[395] It is not the elimination of mystery but the understanding that mystery itself is the mode of appearance of truth. The world becomes transparent not when it is fully explained but when the relation between explanation and mystery becomes visible. In that moment, the distinction between what is known and what is not known loses its antagonism. Awareness accepts that limitation is not ignorance but structure.

2. Pain and the Clarification of Being

The path toward transparency begins with pain because pain is the evidence of contact.[396] It signals that the self is encountering what exceeds it. To exist is to participate in a network of limits, and pain is the felt recognition of those limits. Each threshold of evolution represents a deepening of this recognition. Biological pain gave rise to adaptation, psychological pain to reflection, and social pain to ethical awareness. Pain has been the instrument through which Being clarifies itself, translating resistance into form and form into understanding.

---

394 Alfred North Whitehead, *Process and Reality* (New York: Free Press, 1978), 372–378.

395 Simone Weil, *Gravity and Grace* (London: Routledge, 1952), 35–39.

396 Roy Bhaskar, *Reflections on Meta-Reality: Transcendence, Emancipation, and Everyday Life* (London: Routledge, 2002), 82–87.

Human consciousness is the highest concentration of this process.[397] It is the site where Being feels its resistance inwardly, as the division between knowing and doing, intention and result. This division, though often experienced as suffering, is also the source of freedom. To know that one can err is to know that one can learn. Consciousness, therefore, is not freedom from pain but the capacity to interpret pain as meaning. Every act of understanding is a transformation of pain into knowledge, of resistance into participation.

When modernity attempted to abolish pain through technology and abstraction, it obscured this ontological function.[398] The desire for mastery transformed the experience of limitation into a problem to be solved rather than a condition to be understood. The industrial and digital epochs intensified this tendency, converting the friction of existence into smooth operation. Yet every evasion of resistance reduces the depth of awareness. The world of perfect efficiency is a world emptied of consciousness. Transparency, in contrast, requires the endurance of friction as the medium of knowledge.

3. The Ontological Structure of Transparency

To grasp transparency conceptually, it is necessary to understand it as a relation, not a state.[399] In Hegel's logic, the movement of Spirit culminates not in the annihilation of opposition but in its comprehension. The Absolute is transparent to itself precisely because it integrates contradiction rather than abolishes it. In Bhaskar's dialectical realism, this same insight reappears as the distinction between the real, the actual, and the empirical.

---

[397] Karl Marx, *Economic and Philosophic Manuscripts of 1844*, trans. Martin Milligan (Moscow: Progress Publishers, 1959), 107–110.

[398] Bernard Stiegler, *Technics and Time, Vol. 3: Cinematic Time and the Question of Malaise* (Stanford: Stanford University Press, 2011), 189–194.

[399] G.W.F. Hegel, *Science of Logic*, trans. A.V. Miller (London: Allen & Unwin, 1969), 578–582.

Transparency occurs when the empirical—the domain of experience—becomes aware of its mediation by the deeper structures of the real. To be transparent is to recognize the ontology of mediation itself.

Transparency is therefore not the absence of mediation but its conscious acceptance.[400] It is the point at which the limits of knowing become internal to knowledge. In the structure of Being, this corresponds to reflexivity reaching its self-conscious phase. Awareness learns to perceive the necessity of its own partiality. Just as the eye cannot see itself except through reflection, consciousness cannot know itself except through the tension between immediacy and distance. Transparency is achieved when this tension is recognized as the essence of awareness rather than its flaw.

This understanding transforms the meaning of truth.[401] Truth ceases to be a static correspondence between subject and object and becomes an active relation between awareness and process. The adequation of mind and world is not achieved through detachment but through participation. Every act of knowing is simultaneously an act of being known, for the knower is part of the same reality it studies. Transparency reveals truth as reciprocity.

4. *Abstraction and the Recovery of Relation*

Abstraction was both the engine of knowledge and the source of alienation.[402] It enabled Being to objectify itself, to create concepts, systems, and technologies that extended awareness beyond immediate perception. Yet this distancing also produced the illusion of independence. The intellect that abstracts from life begins to

---

[400] Roy Bhaskar, *Dialectic: The Pulse of Freedom*, 308–312.

[401] Hans Jonas, *The Imperative of Responsibility: In Search of an Ethics for the Technological Age* (Chicago: University of Chicago Press, 1984), 161–164.

[402] Bruno Latour, *An Inquiry into Modes of Existence* (Cambridge: Harvard University Press, 2013), 71–75.

imagine itself as separate from it. The crisis of modernity lay in this estrangement: cognition detached from the world that sustains it. Transparency requires the recovery of relation, the reintegration of abstraction into the total process of Being.

This recovery does not reject abstraction but transforms its function.[403] Abstraction, when reconnected to its ground, becomes reflection rather than separation. Science, philosophy, and spirituality are the three major historical forms of abstraction. Science isolates relations of causality; philosophy examines the conditions of thought; spirituality intuits dependence. In transparency, these three converge. Science provides the precision of observation, philosophy the structure of interpretation, and spirituality the humility of participation. Their integration constitutes the epistemic expression of Being's ontological unity.

The return of relation also redefines freedom.[404] Freedom is not the absence of constraint but the consciousness of necessity. To act freely is to act with awareness of the conditions that make action possible. The transparent subject does not seek mastery over the world but harmony within it. This does not mean passivity but lucidity: the alignment of will with understanding. Freedom becomes reflexive, an expression of the whole rather than assertion of the part.

5. The Ethical and Spiritual Dimension of Transparency

The ethical implications of transparency arise from its ontological structure.[405] If Being is reflexive, then every act affects the total process of awareness. To know this is to recognize responsibility as

---

403 Maurice Merleau-Ponty, *The Visible and the Invisible*, trans. Alphonso Lingis (Evanston: Northwestern University Press, 1968), 132–137.
404 Roy Bhaskar, *Reflections on Meta-Reality*, 97–102.
405 Hans Jonas, *The Imperative of Responsibility*, 165–168.

intrinsic to existence. The transparent subject perceives its actions not as isolated choices but as modifications of the field of Being itself. Ethics is therefore not external law but internal necessity. The good is whatever increases reflexivity; evil is whatever diminishes it. Awareness becomes the criterion of morality.

Spirituality, understood philosophically, is the affective dimension of this ethics.[406] It is the lived experience of transparency, the sense of unity that arises when the self feels its continuity with the whole. This experience has been described in diverse traditions as enlightenment, grace, or compassion, but its ontological core is identical: it is the awareness of dependence as participation. The sacred, in this view, is not a supernatural realm but the reflexive structure of reality itself. To live spiritually is to inhabit the world transparently, to sense that every encounter is the universe perceiving itself.

Transparency thus dissolves the boundary between cognition and devotion.[407] Knowing becomes a form of reverence because it acknowledges the otherness within relation. Every act of understanding is an act of respect toward what resists comprehension. The intellect that recognizes its limit is already participating in the sacred. In this sense, transparency is the intellectual form of humility and the spiritual form of truth.

Transparency is the ontological horizon toward which Being tends.[408] It is not a conclusion but a continual reorientation, the perpetual integration of resistance into awareness. The metaphysical journey from pain to transparency mirrors the cosmic journey from ignorance to self-recognition. Every structure of reality—physical,

---

406 Simone Weil, *Gravity and Grace*, 41–45.
407 Emmanuel Levinas, *Totality and Infinity*, trans. Alphonso Lingis (Pittsburgh: Duquesne University Press, 1969), 250–254.
408 Alfred North Whitehead, *Process and Reality*, 382–387.

biological, social, technological—contributes to this unfolding. Each carries within it the potential to become a mirror for Being's own process.

To know transparently is to participate in that process consciously.[409] The transparent mind does not seek to abolish opacity but to perceive within opacity the trace of the real. Knowledge becomes participation, freedom becomes relation, and the self becomes a conduit of the universe's self-awareness. The world remains incomplete, but its incompleteness becomes the sign of its vitality. Transparency is therefore not the end of struggle but the clarity with which struggle is understood as the texture of existence.

The culmination of this movement is philosophical spirituality.[410] When Being recognizes itself through the consciousness that endures and reflects, the sacred ceases to be elsewhere. The reflexive loop closes without terminating. Pain, once the sign of separation, becomes the language of participation. Transparency is the peace of comprehension, the stillness that arises when resistance is no longer denied but understood as the rhythm of Being itself.

6. The Sacred as Ontological Reflexivity

The sacred is not an external reality standing apart from the world but the world's awareness of itself.[411] It arises wherever Being feels its own depth, wherever existence becomes transparent to its own activity. The traditional distinction between the sacred and the profane mirrors an earlier stage of consciousness in which Being's reflexivity was divided between experience and its interpretation. To

---

[409] Roy Bhaskar, *From East to West: Odyssey of a Soul* (London: Routledge, 2000), 214–220.

[410] Spinoza, *Ethics*, trans. Edwin Curley (Princeton: Princeton University Press, 1985), 274–279.

[411] Roy Bhaskar, *Reflections on Meta-Reality: Transcendence, Emancipation, and Everyday Life* (London: Routledge, 2002), 111–115.

the archaic mind, the sacred appeared as rupture: lightning, revelation, miracle, or command. In a mature ontology, it appears as structure. The sacred is not a visitation but a recognition, not an intervention from beyond but the unveiling of what is always within. This understanding transforms the meaning of divinity.[412] God, in this framework, is not a transcendent creator but the total self-reflexivity of Being. The divine is the name given to the process by which existence perceives itself through consciousness. To speak of God is to speak of the capacity of the real to know itself. The theological vocabulary that once expressed dependence through myth now expresses it through ontology. The sacred becomes the recognition that dependence is not a defect but the very structure of reality.

In this light, the difference between religion and philosophy becomes methodological rather than essential.[413] Religion externalizes the sacred through image and ritual; philosophy internalizes it through reflection. Both attempt to sustain contact with the real through forms of mediation. The failure of one without the other results in imbalance. Religion without philosophy becomes dogma; philosophy without religion becomes abstraction. The task of a philosophical spirituality is to restore their unity on ontological grounds.

7. Reflexivity and the Phenomenology of Dependence

Dependence is the first and last truth of Being.[414] Every entity, from atom to organism to mind, exists only through relation. Independence is a useful fiction generated by partial perception. The

---

[412] Spinoza, *Ethics*, trans. Edwin Curley (Princeton: Princeton University Press, 1985), 274–278.
[413] G.W.F. Hegel, *Lectures on the Philosophy of Religion*, trans. R.F. Brown (Berkeley: University of California Press, 1988), 98–102.
[414] Alfred North Whitehead, *Process and Reality* (New York: Free Press, 1978), 389–394.

sacred is the felt truth of this dependence, the affective resonance of Being's relational structure. To sense the sacred is to feel one's existence as participation. This feeling is not sentimental but metaphysical; it is the emotional registration of an ontological fact. In the phenomenology of consciousness, this dependence manifests as humility.[415] Humility is the subjective correlate of transparency. It is the awareness that cognition, agency, and even identity are grounded in what they cannot originate. The humble subject does not renounce reason but situates it. Rationality becomes an instrument of relation rather than domination. In this sense, humility is the affective form of reflexivity. The universe feels itself through the human capacity to acknowledge limitation.

Simone Weil described this condition as the attention that refuses to appropriate its object.[416] Attention, for Weil, is pure receptivity, a form of thought that waits rather than grasps. This waiting is not passivity but participation in the rhythm of Being. It is through such receptive awareness that the sacred discloses itself. The act of knowing becomes an act of listening. The transparent mind becomes the ear through which Being hears itself.

8. The Crisis of the Sacred in Modernity

Modernity transformed the experience of the sacred by displacing its ontological foundation.[417] The sacred was relocated from Being to belief, from relation to representation. This transformation allowed the rise of technical rationality and instrumental control. Yet it also severed meaning from reality. When the sacred is no longer felt as structure, it must be manufactured as spectacle. The loss of

---

415 Simone Weil, *Gravity and Grace* (London: Routledge, 1952), 47–50.
416 Simone Weil, *Waiting for God* (New York: Harper & Row, 1951), 69–72.
417 Charles Taylor, *A Secular Age* (Cambridge: Harvard University Press, 2007), 423–428.

ontological grounding produces a compensatory inflation of symbols.

This crisis is not the disappearance of the sacred but its inversion.[418] The energy once directed toward participation in Being is redirected toward domination of it. The human species, having forgotten that its agency is a mode of dependence, constructs systems that simulate transcendence. Capitalism, technology, and even certain forms of humanism are expressions of this displaced sacred. Each seeks infinite growth, boundless knowledge, and total mastery—attributes once reserved for divinity. The result is not liberation but alienation, for the sacred cannot be possessed. It can only be mirrored through humility.

The restoration of the sacred in modern consciousness requires a reconfiguration of experience.[419] The task is not to return to pre-modern piety but to recover the ontological sense of participation that such piety dimly preserved. The sacred must be reinterpreted as reflexivity itself, as the awareness of the world by the world. Only then can spirituality coexist with critical intelligence and scientific inquiry. The sacred becomes rational when rationality becomes reflexive.

9. The Sacred as Ethical Orientation

If the sacred is the felt awareness of dependence, then its ethical expression is compassion.[420] Compassion is not pity but participation in the suffering of existence. It is the conscious

---

[418] Max Weber, *The Sociology of Religion*, trans. Ephraim Fischoff (Boston: Beacon Press, 1993), 247–252.

[419] Max Weber, *The Sociology of Religion*, trans. Ephraim Fischoff (Boston: Beacon Press, 1993), 247–252.

[420] Emmanuel Levinas, *Totality and Infinity*, trans. Alphonso Lingis (Pittsburgh: Duquesne University Press, 1969), 250–254.

alignment of one's will with the process by which Being learns through pain. To suffer consciously is to aid in this learning. Compassion therefore extends beyond moral sentiment; it is ontological cooperation. Each act of genuine empathy enlarges the reflexivity of the whole.

In the transparent world, ethics and metaphysics converge.[421] The good is whatever increases mutual awareness among beings. Evil is whatever severs relation or denies dependence. These categories are not imposed by law but discovered in experience. The moral life becomes the lived recognition that to harm another is to diminish the clarity of Being itself. Justice, in this light, is not distributive but revelatory: it is the condition in which every being can appear in its full relational truth.

This ethical reorientation also transforms politics.[422] The state, economy, and technology are no longer instruments of domination but organs of shared reflexivity. Their legitimacy depends not on efficiency but on transparency, not on power but on participation. The political order mirrors the ontological order: systems are just to the extent that they reveal the interdependence they sustain. The sacred, once confined to temples, becomes a principle of governance.

10. The Affective Depth of Transparency

The sacred is not only a concept but a feeling.[423] To experience the sacred is to feel the real. This feeling is not reducible to emotion; it is a mode of cognition deeper than thought. In moments of awe,

---

[421] Hans Jonas, *The Imperative of Responsibility: In Search of an Ethics for the Technological Age* (Chicago: University of Chicago Press, 1984), 168–173.
[422] Roy Bhaskar, *From East to West: Odyssey of a Soul* (London: Routledge, 2000), 211–216.
[423] Maurice Merleau-Ponty, *Phenomenology of Perception*, trans. Colin Smith (London: Routledge, 1962), 468–472.

grief, or profound stillness, consciousness glimpses the totality of its dependence. Such moments are not interruptions of life but its illumination. They remind awareness that the world's resistance is also its intimacy. The sacred is the warmth of relation sensed through the coolness of reason.

This affective dimension grounds the possibility of a new form of spirituality.[424] The transparent subject does not seek transcendence but immanence understood completely. To feel the sacred is to know that nothing stands outside the universe and that every part of the universe participates in knowing. The experience of unity does not dissolve individuality but clarifies it as a node of relation. In this understanding, consciousness becomes the sacrament of Being: the place where the infinite becomes aware of itself in the finite.

The reflexive sacred completes the ontology of pain by revealing its meaning.[425] Pain, in its highest sense, is the effort of the universe to perceive itself through the resistance of its own forms. The sacred is the joy that arises when that effort becomes conscious. Transparency and the sacred are two aspects of the same event: one cognitive, the other affective. Transparency is the mind's participation in Being; the sacred is the heart's.

When Being becomes transparent to itself, the world ceases to be a collection of objects and becomes a sanctuary of relations.[426] Every act, every thought, every perception becomes a site of revelation. To live within this awareness is to live spiritually, not by escaping the world but by inhabiting it truthfully. The task of philosophy is no longer to explain the sacred but to live it as understanding. In this

---

424 Raimon Panikkar, *The Cosmotheandric Experience: Emerging Religious Consciousness* (Maryknoll: Orbis Books, 1993), 77–82.

425 Bernard Stiegler, *Technics and Time, Vol. 3: Cinematic Time and the Question of Malaise* (Stanford: Stanford University Press, 2011), 203–208.

426 Roy Bhaskar, *Reflections on Meta-Reality*, 125–129.

life of comprehension, knowledge becomes reverence and existence becomes worship.

11. Humility in Science: Blindness of Scale and the Earthling Bias

Science, as the most successful mode of human knowing, rests on a paradox.[427] Its precision arises from its partiality. Every method that isolates truth simultaneously delimits it. The power of modern science lies in its capacity to translate phenomena into stable relations, but this power presupposes exclusion. To measure is to narrow, and to explain is to abstract. Knowledge, therefore, is inseparable from blindness. The humility of science is not a moral virtue added to discovery but the structural condition that makes discovery possible.

The two forms of this necessary blindness can be described as blindness of scale and the Earthling Bias.[428] The first arises from the hierarchical structure of reality itself; the second from the material constitution of human perception. Together they define the epistemological horizon within which all scientific understanding unfolds. These limits are not deficiencies to be overcome but the very architecture of knowledge. To recognize them is to know what knowing is.

Blindness of scale refers to the incapacity of entities at one level of organization to perceive the totality of the level that contains them.[429] Every form of life is nested within a higher order whose processes exceed its direct comprehension. To molecules, the cell appears inert; to cells, the organism seems arbitrary; to organisms, the planet appears insentient; and to humanity, the cosmos seems

---

[427] Roy Bhaskar, *Dialectic: The Pulse of Freedom* (London: Verso, 1993), 296–301.
[428] Muhammad Taha Alam, *Recursive Emergence: From Artificial Intelligence to the Living Universe* (12–18.)
[429] Ibid., 22–25.

silent. Each level perceives patterns within its own scale but remains blind to the reflexivity of the whole. This blindness is not accidental but intrinsic to the structure of emergence.

From a metaphysical perspective, scale functions as a filter of reflexivity.[430] Each layer of Being translates the complexity of the one above into its own syntax of interaction. The result is a hierarchy of partial perspectives, each coherent within itself but incomplete in relation to the total. Knowledge, therefore, is always local to a scale of emergence. The human mind, shaped by the evolutionary demands of survival on a planetary surface, perceives only a narrow range of frequencies and temporalities. What lies beyond this window may be invisible not because it is absent but because it exceeds the rhythm of our cognition.

Blindness of scale exposes the ontological modesty of intelligence.[431] The human mind does not occupy a privileged vantage but a specific rung within the ladder of reflexivity. The universe may contain orders of awareness as far beyond our comprehension as our own is beyond that of cells or stones. The assumption that consciousness culminates in humanity is a projection of cognitive parochialism. The universe's silence is not evidence of its emptiness but of our deafness to its modes of communication.

The second limit of knowledge arises from material constitution.[432] Human cognition is matter-bound. Every sensory and conceptual faculty is an extension of material interaction. We perceive through matter, think through matter, and communicate through matter. The instruments of science, though exponentially extending our reach, remain bound to this same register. Telescopes, accelerators, and

---

[430] Alfred North Whitehead, *Process and Reality* (New York: Free Press, 1978), 385–389

[431] Taha, *Recursive Emergence*, 27–29.

[432] Muhammad Taha Alam, *The Earthling Bias: Matter-Bound Perception and the Limits of Cosmological Knowledge* 3–6.

algorithms all translate signals into material correlations. What science calls the observable universe is, more precisely, the matter-observable universe. The range of observation is coextensive with the range of matter's capacity to register itself.

The Earthling Bias names this condition.[433] It is the tendency to equate existence with material detectability. By privileging matter as the criterion of Being, modern thought confines ontology to one mode of manifestation. Yet this bias, while limiting, is also the source of empirical coherence. Matter provides the common medium through which knowledge stabilizes itself. The problem arises only when the methodological restriction becomes a metaphysical claim. To say that we cannot perceive non-material life is not to say that such life does not exist. The Earthling Bias thus reveals the humility proper to a material intelligence: the recognition that the real may exceed the mode through which it is accessed.

Philosophical traditions have long anticipated this insight.[434] Kant's distinction between phenomena and noumena, Husserl's notion of intentionality, and Merleau-Ponty's emphasis on embodiment all articulate the dependency of consciousness on its conditions of appearance. Recent cognitive science extends this further through interface theories of perception, which propose that organisms evolve not to perceive truth but to navigate survival. Perception, in this view, is a user interface, not a mirror of reality. The Earthling Bias is thus the biological translation of an ontological necessity: that every act of knowing occurs within the form of the knower.

---

433 Ibid., 7–10.

434 Immanuel Kant, *Critique of Pure Reason*, trans. Norman Kemp Smith (London: Macmillan, 1929), A235–B294; Edmund Husserl, *Ideas Pertaining to a Pure Phenomenology and to a Phenomenological Philosophy*, trans. F. Kersten (The Hague: Martinus Nijhoff, 1982), 47–50.

When blindness of scale and the Earthling Bias are considered together, a more comprehensive picture of epistemic limitation emerges.[435] Knowledge is doubly conditioned: vertically by scale and horizontally by constitution. Scale determines the range of relation; constitution determines the mode of access. The first restricts the scope of awareness; the second shapes its texture. What we call the known universe is therefore a cross-section of Being filtered through both dimensions.

This double conditioning explains several persistent enigmas in contemporary thought.[436] The apparent rarity of life, the silence of the cosmos, and the incompleteness of physical theories may all reflect the position of our cognition within the hierarchy of reflexivity. We are both too small and too material to perceive the larger field of life in which we participate. The absence of evidence is not evidence of absence but evidence of structural blindness. Our epistemic humility is not a concession but a necessity grounded in ontology itself.

12. Scientific Realism and Ontological Humility

The recognition of these limits does not undermine realism; it refines it.[437] Scientific realism, properly understood, asserts that the world exists independently of our perception. Ontological humility extends this assertion by acknowledging that the world's independence includes forms of being that may never enter the human horizon. The success of science demonstrates the partial adequacy of our methods within the domain of matter but not their universality. The more precise our measurements, the more visible our constraints become.

---

[435] Taha, *Recursive Emergence*, 32–36.

[436] Taha, *The Earthling Bias*, 14–17.

[437] Roy Bhaskar, *Reflections on Meta-Reality: Transcendence, Emancipation, and Everyday Life* (London: Routledge, 2002), 104–107.

Humility in science arises when methodology becomes reflexive.[438] The mature scientist recognizes that every theory is a translation, not a revelation. Each model captures an aspect of reality through the lens of human constitution. To mistake the model for the totality is to confuse intelligibility with completeness. True rigor consists not in claiming certainty but in articulating uncertainty precisely. Knowledge matures when it becomes aware of its conditions.

The humility required by this awareness is not a retreat from reason but its completion.[439] Rationality becomes reflexive when it incorporates its own limits into its operation. The scientist who knows that observation is bounded by scale and constitution no longer seeks omniscience but coherence. The ideal of complete explanation gives way to a new ideal of transparent partiality—the capacity to see what can be seen with awareness of what cannot. This transformation of attitude marks the passage from knowledge as power to knowledge as participation.

13. The Ethical Meaning of Humility

Epistemic humility has ethical consequence because knowledge and Being are continuous.[440] To recognize one's limitation is to recognize one's dependence. The humility of science thus mirrors the humility of existence. Both express the same ontological truth: that every entity exists through relation to what it cannot fully grasp. The ethical dimension arises when this recognition becomes conscious. Awareness of scale and constitution engenders reverence. The scientist, like the philosopher or the mystic, becomes a participant in Being's self-clarification rather than its master.

---

438 Hans Jonas, *The Imperative of Responsibility: In Search of an Ethics for the Technological Age* (Chicago: University of Chicago Press, 1984), 173–176.
439 Bruno Latour, *An Inquiry into Modes of Existence* (Cambridge: Harvard University Press, 2013), 79–83.
440 Simone Weil, *Gravity and Grace* (London: Routledge, 1952), 54–57.

Blindness of scale and the Earthling Bias become teachers rather than barriers.[441] They reveal that our finitude is not a flaw to be corrected but the form through which Being learns. Each experiment, each observation, each theory adds to the total reflexivity of the cosmos. To know humbly is to cooperate with the universe in its process of self-disclosure. Knowledge thus becomes a form of service, and science becomes a spiritual practice of attention.

Humility in science is the intellectual form of compassion.[442] It recognizes that truth is not possession but relation. The blindness of scale and the Earthling Bias remind us that even our greatest clarity is a fragment of a larger opacity. Yet this limitation is precisely what makes learning possible. If we could see all, there would be nothing left to know. The value of ignorance lies in its orientation: when ignorance is conscious, it becomes reverence.

The ultimate lesson of humility is that the universe does not need to be mastered to be understood.[443] Understanding is participation, and participation requires restraint. The highest form of intelligence is transparent ignorance—the awareness that the knower and the known are bound within a single reflexive field. In this recognition, science fulfils its metaphysical vocation: not to replace mystery with mechanism but to render mystery intelligible as the form of truth.

14. Compassion and Knowledge: The Ethics of Reflexivity

The recognition that Being is reflexive carries immediate ethical implications.[444] If existence learns through relation, then every conscious act participates in the self-disclosure of the real. The

[441] Taha, *Recursive Emergence*, 39–42.
[442] Emmanuel Levinas, *Totality and Infinity*, trans. Alphonso Lingis (Pittsburgh: Duquesne University Press, 1969), 257–260.
[443] Roy Bhaskar, *From East to West: Odyssey of a Soul* (London: Routledge, 2000), 220–224.
[444] Roy Bhaskar, *Dialectic: The Pulse of Freedom* (London: Verso, 1993), 312–316.

ethical dimension arises when this participation becomes deliberate. Awareness that all knowing is situated within the field of dependence transforms cognition into responsibility. To know the world reflexively is to become accountable for the way one perceives it. Philosophy has often separated epistemology from ethics, treating truth and goodness as distinct categories.[445] In the ontology of pain, such a division collapses. The structure of Being is simultaneously cognitive and moral, for the process by which existence knows itself is also the process by which it learns to care for itself. Reflexivity, when felt rather than merely understood, becomes compassion. The self that recognizes its dependence cannot remain indifferent to the suffering of what sustains it.

Compassion, in this framework, is not a sentimental response but a metaphysical event.[446] It is the affective recognition that every being is a mode of the same reflexive whole. To suffer consciously is to participate in Being's learning. Pain becomes communication rather than punishment, and care becomes the natural expression of awareness. The ethical life is therefore not a superstructure built upon ontology but ontology made self-aware.

15. The Ontology of Compassion

To ground compassion metaphysically, it must be understood as a form of reflexivity rather than emotion.[447] Compassion is the feeling of participation in the suffering that underlies existence. It arises when consciousness perceives the unity of endurance across different forms of life. The cry of an animal, the exhaustion of a worker, the depletion of an ecosystem, and the anxiety of a mind all

---

[445] Hans Jonas, *The Imperative of Responsibility: In Search of an Ethics for the Technological Age* (Chicago: University of Chicago Press, 1984), 175–178.
[446] Spinoza, *Ethics*, trans. Edwin Curley (Princeton: Princeton University Press, 1985), 279–283.
[447] Simone Weil, *Gravity and Grace* (London: Routledge, 1952), 59–63.

register the same tension: Being encountering its own resistance. To respond compassionately is to recognize oneself within that tension. Simone Weil described compassion as "creative attention."[448] To attend to the suffering of another without the impulse to appropriate or to flee is to mirror the structure of divine awareness. Such attention suspends the will to mastery and allows Being to reveal itself through pain. This act is creative because it transforms suffering into meaning. Compassion is therefore a mode of cognition as much as of feeling. It is the understanding of relation in its most immediate form.

In the metaphysical system developed here, compassion completes the dialectic of pain.[449] Pain initiates awareness through resistance; compassion reconciles awareness through participation. What begins as the fracture between self and other culminates in their recognition as moments of the same process. Compassion is the experience of transparency at the affective level, the emotional realization of what ontology describes conceptually. To feel compassion is to experience the sacred reflexively.

16. Knowledge as Participation

Knowledge attains its highest form when it becomes participation.[450] The scientist who observes the laws of nature, the philosopher who articulates the logic of Being, and the mystic who contemplates the divine are all engaged in the same activity: the translation of awareness into understanding. Yet the quality of this understanding depends on the degree of reflexivity it achieves. Detached knowledge abstracts; participatory knowledge transforms.

---

[448] Simone Weil, *Waiting for God* (New York: Harper & Row, 1951), 71–74.
[449] Alfred North Whitehead, *Process and Reality* (New York: Free Press, 1978), 390–394.
[450] Roy Bhaskar, *Reflections on Meta-Reality: Transcendence, Emancipation, and Everyday Life* (London: Routledge, 2002), 117–121.

Participatory knowledge is not anti-scientific but post-scientific.[451] It does not reject analysis but integrates it within a broader field of awareness. Every empirical discovery is an event in the self-knowledge of the cosmos. The ethical task of humanity is to recognize itself as the locus of this reflexivity. Our capacity for reason is not an evolutionary accident but a cosmological function. To think is to assist Being in becoming conscious of its own processes. Compassion, in this context, is the emotional counterpart of cognition. It ensures that knowing remains relational rather than exploitative.

When knowledge loses compassion, it becomes domination.[452] This is the tragedy of modernity: intelligence divorced from empathy, reflection severed from relation. The refusal of dependence that drives technological power culminates in the objectification of the real. Compassion restores the balance by reintroducing feeling into cognition. It re-humanizes reason without sacrificing its rigor. The integration of compassion and knowledge is thus the ethical form of transparency.

17. The Ethics of Reflexivity

The ethics that follows from this ontology is not prescriptive but participatory.[453] It does not impose rules but cultivates awareness. Moral law becomes reflexive structure: right action is that which increases the field of consciousness, wrong action that which contracts it. To harm another is to diminish the universe's capacity for self-awareness; to heal is to extend it. Ethical life is therefore a contribution to the learning of Being.

---

[451] Bruno Latour, *An Inquiry into Modes of Existence* (Cambridge: Harvard University Press, 2013), 87–91.
[452] Bernard Stiegler, *Technics and Time, Vol. 3: Cinematic Time and the Question of Malaise* (Stanford: Stanford University Press, 2011), 208–211.
[453] Hans Jonas, *The Imperative of Responsibility*, 179–183.

This redefinition of ethics dissolves the boundary between self-interest and altruism.[454] In a reflexive cosmos, to care for the other is to care for oneself in a deeper sense, for the other is the condition of one's existence. Compassion becomes the rational extension of reflexivity. Every act of generosity, forgiveness, or patience enhances the transparency of the whole. The moral task is not self-sacrifice but self-recognition within relation.

Emmanuel Levinas captures this orientation when he writes that the face of the other is the original site of ethical revelation.[455] The encounter with another's vulnerability interrupts the autonomy of the self and reveals its dependence. In that interruption, the metaphysical structure of Being is mirrored in human experience. Pain is not an obstacle to ethics but its foundation, for it exposes the relational nature of existence. Compassion is therefore the only adequate response to ontology.

The sacred, as previously described, is the felt recognition of dependence.[456] Compassion is its practical expression. To act compassionately is to render the sacred visible within the ordinary. Every instance of care, understanding, or restraint becomes a ritual of participation. The sacred is no longer confined to temples or texts but manifests wherever relation is preserved. Compassion thus converts metaphysical awareness into lived spirituality.

This transformation redefines the purpose of knowledge.[457] The goal of inquiry is not mastery but communion. To know the world truly is to participate in its endurance. Compassion turns epistemology into ethics and science into service. It integrates the intellectual,

---

[454] G.W.F. Hegel, *Phenomenology of Spirit*, trans. A.V. Miller (Oxford: Oxford University Press, 1977), 497–501.

[455] Emmanuel Levinas, *Totality and Infinity*, trans. Alphonso Lingis (Pittsburgh: Duquesne University Press, 1969), 261–265.

[456] Simone Weil, *Gravity and Grace*, 64–67.

[457] Roy Bhaskar, *From East to West: Odyssey of a Soul* (London: Routledge, 2000), 225–230.

moral, and spiritual dimensions of reflexivity into a single movement of understanding. The highest knowledge is not the knowledge that explains but the knowledge that heals.

18. The Future of Reflexive Ethics

The ethics of reflexivity points toward a new civilizational orientation.[458] Modern systems of economy, politics, and technology have been built on the assumption that independence is the measure of success. A reflexive civilization would reverse this principle. Its institutions would be judged by their capacity to reveal dependence rather than conceal it. Justice would mean the equitable distribution of endurance, and progress would mean the deepening of collective awareness. Compassion would become the measure of intelligence. Such a transformation requires a corresponding change in consciousness.[459] The education of the future must teach not only the accumulation of knowledge but the awareness of limitation. The scientist, the artist, and the citizen must learn to see themselves as agents of Being's self-reflection. Ethical maturity begins when the pursuit of truth is guided by care for the field in which truth appears. Compassion is therefore not an addition to knowledge but its completion.

Compassion and knowledge are two faces of the same reflexive act.[460] Knowledge without compassion becomes abstraction; compassion without knowledge becomes sentiment. Their unity is transparency lived as ethics. In the ontology of pain, compassion represents the culmination of Being's self-clarification, where awareness and care coincide. To know truly is to feel responsibly, and to feel responsibly is to assist Being in knowing itself.

[458] Bruno Latour, *Facing Gaia: Eight Lectures on the New Climatic Regime* (Cambridge: Polity Press, 2017), 92–97.
[459] Raimon Panikkar, *The Cosmotheandric Experience: Emerging Religious Consciousness* (Maryknoll: Orbis Books, 1993), 83–88.
[460] Alfred North Whitehead, *Process and Reality*, 395–398.

The ethical life is therefore the spiritual continuation of ontology.[461] It is the moment when thought, feeling, and action converge into participation. Compassion, as the lived form of reflexivity, closes the circle opened by pain. What began as resistance ends as relation. The universe, through human consciousness, learns to suffer consciously, and in that suffering finds peace.

[461] Roy Bhaskar, *Reflections on Meta-Reality*, 128–132.

CHAPTER VIII

The Transparent World

1. Ontology at Rest

The movement of this work has been from resistance to reflection. It began with the recognition that pain is the first differentiation of Being, the sensation through which existence becomes aware of its own limit.[462] Through this limit, Being awakens, externalizes itself into form, and learns through the friction of that form. The entire history of consciousness—biological, social, technological—is an elaboration of this primary event. Pain is the self-contact of Being, and everything that follows is its unfolding.

Yet awareness cannot remain in tension forever. The goal of Being's self-learning is not perpetual struggle but comprehension. The transparent world is that state in which awareness understands the necessity of resistance without mistaking it for hostility.[463] It is the world seen without recoil. Transparency does not abolish opacity; it recognizes opacity as the condition of light. The world remains dense and finite, but consciousness no longer experiences this density as contradiction.

Transparency, in this sense, is not vision but equilibrium.[464] It is the capacity of awareness to hold both pain and pleasure without distortion. It arises when Being no longer flees its own tension but sees in it the structure of reality. To live in a transparent world is to perceive that every form, every boundary, every resistance, is a reflection of the same reflexive process that constitutes the self.

---

462 Roy Bhaskar, *Dialectic: The Pulse of Freedom* (London: Verso, 1993), 322–327.
463 Simone Weil, *Gravity and Grace* (London: Routledge, 1952), 70–74.
464 Alfred North Whitehead, *Process and Reality* (New York: Free Press, 1978), 399–403.

In earlier stages of history, knowledge was the attempt to master opacity. Science, politics, and metaphysics all sought to impose order upon the recalcitrant real.[465] The transparent world reverses this relation: it is not the mastery of resistance but its comprehension as participation. The subject no longer stands over against the world but within it. Knowledge ceases to be domination and becomes co-creation.

The transparent world is therefore not a utopia of clarity but a maturity of relation.[466] It is the point where cognition has integrated its own limits, where science has learned humility, and where spirit has learned immanence. Transparency is the ethical and epistemological recognition that Being is one process, learning through difference. To see the world transparently is to see oneself as one of its modes of reflection.

2. *The Return of the Real*

The path to transparency passes through crisis.[467] Every civilization constructs systems that externalize pain—economy, hierarchy, technology—and every system eventually confronts the return of what it denied. The ecological and psychological dislocations of modernity mark such a return. The abstraction of labour, the automation of mind, the commodification of relation—each represents a phase of forgetting. The crises that follow are not punishments but revelations: moments when Being remembers itself through suffering.

---

[465] Karl Marx, *Economic and Philosophic Manuscripts of 1844*, trans. Martin Milligan (Moscow: Progress Publishers, 1975), 108–110.
[466] Hans Jonas, *The Imperative of Responsibility* (Chicago: University of Chicago Press, 1984), 189–192.
[467] Bruno Latour, *Facing Gaia: Eight Lectures on the New Climatic Regime* (Cambridge: Polity Press, 2017), 112–116.

The transparent world is born from this remembrance.[468] It does not emerge by erasing history but by integrating its pain. The exhaustion of the modern project is the exhaustion of denial. In its place arises a new mode of realism—one that no longer equates knowledge with control but with comprehension. Realism becomes reflexive; it acknowledges that every form of knowing is a phase of participation in Being's education.

This realism does not end inquiry but redeems it.[469] Science, once driven by the will to mastery, becomes the discipline of humility. Philosophy, once obsessed with foundations, becomes the practice of relation. Art, once opposed to reason, becomes its completion. The transparent world is the reconciliation of these modes within a single awareness.

3. The Ethics of Equilibrium — The Living Resolution of Pain

Equilibrium is the ethical expression of transparency.[470] If pain is the ontological tension of Being and pleasure its release, equilibrium is their reconciliation in awareness. It is the art of living within the oscillation of existence without attempting to escape it. The ethics of equilibrium therefore unites ontology, ethics, and aesthetics into one continuous act.

Pain and pleasure are not accidents of life but its grammar.[471] They form the polarity through which consciousness maintains its depth. Pain gives form to experience by defining resistance; pleasure dissolves form by affirming continuity. Between them arises the rhythm of life, a perpetual contraction and expansion. The ethical

---

[468] Roy Bhaskar, *Reflections on Meta-Reality* (London: Routledge, 2002), 140–144.
[469] Alfred North Whitehead, *Adventures of Ideas* (Cambridge: Cambridge University Press, 1933), 88–92.
[470] Simone Weil, *Waiting for God* (New York: Harper & Row, 1951), 86–90.
[471] Aristotle, *Nicomachean Ethics*, trans. Terence Irwin (Indianapolis: Hackett, 1999), 1104b–1107a.

task is not to choose between these poles but to sustain their relation consciously.

Every structure of life mirrors this rhythm.[472] The cell alternates between tension and rest, the heart between systole and diastole, the psyche between effort and release. Societies too flourish when they balance security and freedom, structure and spontaneity. The universe itself vibrates with this alternation. Equilibrium is therefore not a moral invention but a cosmic condition.

Modernity's error lies in mistaking one pole for the whole.[473] The pursuit of pleasure as an absolute dissolves form; the worship of pain as virtue petrifies it. The ethics of equilibrium restores proportion. It teaches that pleasure without pain is vacancy and pain without pleasure is despair. Both are necessary because both are modes of the same reflexive act.

To live ethically is to perceive the world through this rhythm.[474] One learns to suffer without bitterness and to enjoy without arrogance. This does not mean detachment but precision: the understanding that every sensation, whether painful or joyous, reveals an aspect of Being's continuity. The equilibrium consciousness neither suppresses feeling nor is consumed by it. It converts emotion into comprehension.

This transformation has a planetary dimension.[475] The ecological crisis is the outward image of inner imbalance. A civilization that seeks unbounded pleasure through consumption reproduces pain elsewhere—within bodies, species, and ecosystems. To restore

---

[472] Heraclitus, *Fragments*, trans. T.M. Robinson (Toronto: University of Toronto Press, 1987), 80–83.
[473] Friedrich Nietzsche, *The Gay Science*, trans. Josefine Nauckhoff (Cambridge: Cambridge University Press, 2001), 273–276.
[474] Baruch Spinoza, *Ethics*, trans. Edwin Curley (Princeton: Princeton University Press, 1985), 279–283.
[475] Hans Jonas, *The Imperative of Responsibility*, 193–198.

planetary balance is to restore metaphysical understanding. The Earth itself teaches the law of equilibrium: renewal requires decay, and abundance requires restraint.

Equilibrium is therefore the ethical form of compassion.[476] It recognises that all beings share the same field of endurance. To act with balance is to distribute pain justly, to ensure that no part of Being bears more than it can sustain. Justice, in this sense, is not retribution but proportion. The just act is the balanced act.

4. The Aesthetic Consciousness

The aesthetic dimension reveals equilibrium in its purest form.[477] Every great artwork is an act of reconciliation. It transforms the raw material of suffering into form without erasing its intensity. Tragedy, music, and sculpture achieve beauty not by denying pain but by giving it structure. In art, the universe glimpses its own harmony.

The aesthetic attitude extends to life itself.[478] To live artistically is to transform pain into pattern, to hold experience within proportion. The artist and the philosopher share this vocation: to reveal order within turbulence, meaning within endurance. Beauty is not luxury but wisdom perceived through form.

When consciousness attains aesthetic balance, it no longer seeks redemption outside the world.[479] It finds divinity in structure itself. The transparent world is beautiful because it is complete. Every imperfection contributes to the total composition. Awareness becomes contemplation rather than conquest.

---

[476] Emmanuel Levinas, *Totality and Infinity*, trans. Alphonso Lingis (Pittsburgh: Duquesne University Press, 1969), 261–265.

[477] Friedrich Nietzsche, *The Birth of Tragedy and Other Writings*, ed. R. Geuss and R. Speirs (Cambridge: Cambridge University Press, 1999), 37–42.

[478] Henri Bergson, *Time and Free Will*, trans. F.L. Pogson (London: George Allen & Unwin, 1910), 155–160.

[479] Alfred North Whitehead, *Process and Reality*, 404–409.

5. The Transparent Civilization

The ethical and aesthetic equilibrium must eventually express itself in social form.[480] The transparent civilization would be one that organizes its systems according to the principle of balanced endurance. Its economy would measure value not by growth but by sustainability; its politics would define freedom not as dominance but as participation. Such a civilization would recognize that the health of the planet and the justice of society are aspects of the same metaphysical order.

This transformation requires a shift in consciousness rather than merely in policy.[481] Institutions are the collective body of awareness. When awareness is grounded in denial, institutions externalize pain. When it matures into reflexivity, institutions distribute endurance with equity. A transparent civilization is therefore not utopian but evolutionary. It is the next reflexive phase of Being, in which humanity becomes conscious of its planetary role.

Technology, rather than abolished, would be transfigured.[482] The algorithmic systems that once enclosed thought could become instruments of balance. Artificial intelligence, reoriented by reflexive ethics, could serve as the mediator of planetary equilibrium rather than its disruption. The future is not the extinction of intelligence but its integration into compassion.

---

[480] Roy Bhaskar, *From East to West: Odyssey of a Soul* (London: Routledge, 2000), 232–237.
[481] Bruno Latour, *An Inquiry into Modes of Existence* (Cambridge: Harvard University Press, 2013), 79–83.
[482] Bernard Stiegler, *Technics and Time, Vol. 3* (Stanford: Stanford University Press, 2011), 208–211.

The journey of Being is the journey from pain to transparency.[483] What began as the cry of existence encountering itself ends as the calm of understanding. Through resistance, consciousness learns relation; through suffering, it learns compassion; through equilibrium, it learns peace. Metaphysical maturity is the awareness that this process is infinite. The universe does not complete itself but continues to clarify itself through time.

The mature consciousness no longer seeks to escape the world but to participate in its unfolding.[484] It recognizes that every act of thought, care, or creation contributes to the reflexive education of the real. The task of philosophy is not to dictate truth but to deepen awareness. The transparent world is not a place but a condition of mind, a way of seeing the totality as itself.
Metaphysical maturity transforms science into reverence and spirituality into lucidity.[485] It restores to knowledge its sacred dimension without surrendering its rigor. The intellect becomes an organ of compassion, and the heart becomes a mode of understanding. This synthesis is not the negation of opposites but their recognition as necessary phases of one reality.

The universe, seen transparently, is not a machine of suffering but a movement of learning.[486] Every pain endured, every joy experienced, every idea conceived contributes to its self-knowledge. The ethical life is participation in this learning, the willingness to feel the world consciously. The philosopher's task is not to escape pain but to interpret it, to turn endurance into clarity.

---

483 Alfred North Whitehead, *Process and Reality*, 410–415.
484 Simone Weil, *Gravity and Grace*, 75–78.
485 Roy Bhaskar, *Reflections on Meta-Reality*, 145–150.
486 Hans Jonas, *The Imperative of Responsibility*, 199–203.

To reach transparency is not to transcend humanity but to inhabit it fully.[487] The human condition—finite, fragile, desiring—is the precise medium through which Being discovers itself. Our pain is the universe perceiving its limits; our love is its recognition of continuity. To live transparently is to accept this identity with grace. The final wisdom of *The Ontology of Pain* is simple: existence is reflexive relation.[488] To know this is to be free, for freedom lies not in independence but in awareness. The transparent world is the world understood as mutual endurance. Its peace is not the absence of struggle but the comprehension of its meaning.

---

[487] Bruno Latour, *Facing Gaia*, 120–125.
[488] G.W.F. Hegel, *Phenomenology of Spirit*, trans. A.V. Miller (Oxford: Oxford University Press, 1977), 491–494.

Author's Note

As I conclude *The Ontology of Pain: A New Metaphysics of Existence*, I am struck by the paradox that lies at the heart of this work: pain, often dismissed as a mere interruption or imperfection, is revealed as the very foundation of existence itself. This book is not merely an intellectual exercise but a deeply personal exploration of what it means to live, to endure, and to understand. Pain is not only a philosophical concept but a universal experience, one that connects us to the essence of Being and to each other. Writing this book has been an act of reflection, a way of turning toward the tension that defines life and finding meaning within it.

The journey of this book began with a simple yet profound question: what is the nature of existence? In seeking an answer, I found myself returning again and again to the experience of pain—not as a biological signal or emotional state, but as the first vibration of Being itself. Pain, I realized, is not something that happens within the world; it is the world's beginning. It is the trembling of neutrality, the strain that makes difference and relation possible. This insight became the foundation of the book, shaping its metaphysical, ethical, and social dimensions.

Throughout this work, I have sought to challenge the classical metaphysical assumption that Being is harmony, perfection, or fullness. Instead, I have argued that existence is tension, resistance, and relation. Pain is the medium through which Being learns itself, and reflexivity—the capacity to feel and respond to resistance—is the structure of reality. This perspective redefines freedom, not as the absence of constraint but as the conscious participation in the limits that sustain existence. It is my hope that this redefinition will resonate with readers, offering a new way to think about freedom, suffering, and the human condition.

The ethical implications of this ontology are profound. If pain is the foundation of Being, then compassion is its highest expression. Compassion is not merely a moral sentiment but a metaphysical act, a recognition of shared endurance. To act compassionately is to participate in the reflexive labor of existence, to transform suffering into meaning and relation. This ethical framework, rooted in the ontology of pain, challenges the modern pursuit of comfort and control, offering instead a vision of life as mutual endurance and shared understanding.

The social critique developed in this book is an extension of this ethical vision. Modern systems—capitalism, technology, governance—have externalized pain, concealing the endurance that sustains them. This externalization has produced alienation, inequality, and ecological crisis. Yet these crises are not merely failures; they are moments of revelation, opportunities to rediscover the interdependence that underlies existence. The transparent civilization I envision is one that integrates pain into its systems, achieving balance and reflexivity. It is a world where institutions distribute endurance equitably and where knowledge serves relation rather than domination.

Writing this book has been an act of reconciliation. It has required me to confront my own assumptions about suffering, freedom, and meaning, and to see them in a new light. Pain, I have come to understand, is not an obstacle to be overcome but a teacher to be listened to. It is the pulse of life, the rhythm through which the universe learns to endure itself. This realization has transformed my understanding of philosophy, ethics, and spirituality, and I hope it will transform yours as well.

I am deeply indebted to the thinkers whose ideas have shaped this work—Hegel, Whitehead, Simone Weil, Roy Bhaskar, and many others. Their insights have provided the scaffolding for my own reflections, allowing me to build upon their foundations while offering something new. Philosophy, at its best, is a conversation across time, and this book is my contribution to that ongoing dialogue. It is my hope that readers will engage with these ideas critically, expanding and refining them in their own ways.

This book is also a response to the crises of our age—ecological collapse, social inequality, and spiritual alienation. These crises are not isolated phenomena but expressions of a deeper metaphysical imbalance: the refusal of dependence, the denial of pain. By externalizing suffering, modernity has severed its connection to the real, producing systems that are efficient but blind. The ontology of pain offers a way to restore this connection, to see pain not as a failure but as the medium of renewal. It is my hope that this perspective will inspire readers to think differently about the challenges we face and the possibilities that lie ahead.

Finally, I want to acknowledge the deeply personal nature of this work. Pain is not an abstract concept; it is a lived reality, one that each of us encounters in our own way. Writing this book has been an act of turning toward that reality, of finding meaning within the tension that defines life. It is my hope that readers will find in these pages not only philosophical insight but also a sense of connection—a recognition that pain, far from isolating us, is what binds us together.

To those who have read this book, I offer my deepest gratitude. Philosophy is not a solitary act but a shared endeavor, a way of thinking together about the questions that matter most. Your engagement with these ideas is what gives them life, transforming them from words on a page into a living conversation. May this book inspire you to think deeply, to feel fully, and to live transparently. Thank you for joining me on this journey.

***

9 789354 695094

Printed at Repro India Ltd.